Nutshell Series

of

WEST PUBLISHING COMPANY

P.O. Box 3526

St. Paul, Minnesota 55165

March, 1980

Administrative Law and Process, 1972, 336 pages, by Ernest Gellhorn, Professor of Law, University of Virginia.

Agency-Partnership, 1977, 364 pages, by Roscoe T. Steffen, Late Professor of Law, University of Chicago.

Antitrust Law and Economics, 1976, 406 pages, by Ernest Gellhorn, Professor of Law, University of Virginia.

Civil Procedure, 1979, 271 pages, by Mary Kay Kane, Professor of Law, University of California, Hastings College of the Law.

Civil Rights, 1978, 279 pages, by Norman Vieira, Professor of Law, University of Idaho.

Commercial Paper, 2nd Ed., 1975, 361 pages, by Charles M. Weber, Professor of Business Law, University of Arizona.

Conflicts, 3rd Ed., 1974, 432 pages, by Albert A. Ehrenzweig, Late Professor of Law, University of California, Berkeley.

Constitutional Analysis, 1979, 388 pages, by Jerre S Williams, Professor of Law, University of Texas.

Constitutional Power—Federal and State, 1974, 411 pages, by David E. Engdahl, Professor of Law, University of Denver.

Consumer Protection, 1976, 322 pages, by David G. Epstein, Dean and Professor of Law, University of Arkansas.

Contracts, 1975, 307 pages, by Gordon D. Schaber, Dean and Professor of Law, McGeorge School of Law and Claude D. Rohwer, Professor of Law, McGeorge School of Law.

Corrections and Prisoners' Rights—Law of, 1976, 353 pages, by Sheldon Krantz, Professor of Law, Boston University.

Criminal Law, 1975, 302 pages, by Arnold H. Loewy, Professor of Law, University of North Carolina.

Criminal Procedure—Constitutional Limitations, 2nd Ed., 1975, 404 pages, by Jerold H. Israel, Professor of Law, University of Michigan and Wayne LaFave, Professor of Law, University of Illinois.

Debtor-Creditor Law, 2nd Ed., 1980, 324 pages, by David G. Epstein, Dean and Professor of Law, University of Arkansas.

Employment Discrimination—Federal Law of, 1976, 336 pages, by Mack A. Player, Professor of Law, University of Georgia.

Estate Planning—Introduction to, 2nd Ed., 1978, 378 pages, by Robert J. Lynn, Professor of Law, Ohio State University.

Evidence, 1970, 406 pages, by Paul F. Rothstein, Professor of Law, Georgetown University.

Family Law, 1977, 400 pages, by Harry D. Krause, Professor of Law, University of Illinois.

Federal Estate and Gift Taxation, 2nd Ed., 1979, 488 pages, by John K. McNulty, Professor of Law, University of California, Berkeley.

Federal Income Taxation of Individuals, 2nd Ed., 1978, 422 pages, by John K. McNulty, Professor of Law, University of California, Berkeley.

Federal Income Taxation of Corporations and Stockholders, 1978, 374 pages, by Jonathan Sobeloff, Late Professor of Law, Georgetown University.

Federal Jurisdiction, 1976, 228 pages, by David P. Currie, Professor of Law, University of Chicago.

Government Contracts, 1979, 423 pages, by W. Noel Keyes, Professor of Law, Pepperdine University.

Historical Introduction to Anglo-American Law, 2nd Ed., 1973, 280 pages, by Frederick G. Kempin, Jr., Professor of Business Law, Wharton School of Finance and Commerce, University of Pennsylvania.

Injunctions, 1974, 264 pages, by John F. Dobbyn, Professor of Law, Villanova University.

Judicial Process, (May, 1980), approx. 305 pages, by William L. Reynolds, Professor of Law, University of Maryland.

Jurisdiction, 4th Ed., 1980, approx. 204 pages, by Albert A. Ehrenzweig, Late Professor of Law, University of California, Berkeley, David W. Louisell, Late Professor of Law, University of California, Berkeley and Geoffrey C. Hazard, Jr., Professor of Law, Yale Law School.

Juvenile Courts, 2nd Ed., 1977, 275 pages, by Sanford J. Fox, Professor of Law, Boston College.

Labor Arbitration Law and Practice, 1979, 358 pages, by Dennis R. Nolan, Professor of Law, University of South Carolina.

Labor Law, 1979, 403 pages, by Douglas L. Leslie, Professor of Law, University of Virginia.

Land Use, 1978, 316 pages, by Robert R. Wright, Professor of Law, University of Arkansas, Little Rock and Susan Webber, Professor of Law, University of Arkansas, Little Rock.

Landlord and Tenant Law, 1979, 319 pages, by David S. Hill, Professor of Law, University of Colorado.

Law Study and Law Examinations—Introduction to, 1971, 389 pages, by Stanley V. Kinyon, Late Professor of Law, University of Minnesota.

Legal Interviewing and Counseling, 1976, 353 pages, by Thomas L. Shaffer, Professor of Law, University of Notre Dame.

Legal Research, 3rd Ed., 1978, 415 pages, by Morris L. Cohen, Professor of Law and Law Librarian, Harvard University.

Legislative Law and Process, 1975, 279 pages, by Jack Davies, Professor of Law, William Mitchell College of Law.

Local Government Law, 1975, 386 pages, by David J. McCarthy, Jr., Dean and Professor of Law, Georgetown University.

Mass Communications Law, 1977, 431 pages, by Harvey L. Zuckman, Professor of Law, Catholic University and Martin J. Gaynes, of the Washington, D.C. Bar.

Medical Malpractice—The Law of, 1977, 340 pages, by Joseph H. King, Professor of Law, University of Tennessee.

Military Law, (March, 1980), approx. 379 pages, by Charles A. Shanor, Professor of Law, Emory University and Timothy P. Terrell, Professor of Law, Emory University.

Post-Conviction Remedies, 1978, 360 pages, by Robert Popper, Professor of Law, University of Missouri, Kansas City.

Presidential Power, 1977, 328 pages, by Arthur Selwyn Miller, Professor of Law, George Washington University.

Procedure Before Trial, 1972, 258 pages, by Delmar Karlen, Professor of Law Emeritus, New York University.

Products Liability, 1974, 365 pages, by Dix W. Noel, Late Professor of Law, University of Tennessee and Jerry J. Phillips, Professor of Law, University of Tennessee.

Real Estate Finance, 1979, 292 pages, by Jon W. Bruce, Professor of Law, Stetson University.

Real Property, 1975, 425 pages, by Roger H. Bernhardt, Professor of Law, Golden Gate University.

Remedies, 1977, 364 pages, by John F. O'Connell, Professor of Law, Western State University College of Law.

Res Judicata, 1976, 310 pages, by Robert C. Casad, Professor of Law, University of Kansas.

Secured Transactions, 1976, 377 pages, by Henry J. Bailey, Professor of Law, Willamette University.

Securities Regulation, 1978, 300 pages, by David L. Ratner, Professor of Law, Cornell University.

Titles—The Calculus of Interests, 1968, 277 pages, by Oval A. Phipps, Late Professor of Law, St. Louis University.

Torts—Injuries to Persons and Property, 1977, 434 pages by Edward J. Kionka, Professor of Law, Southern Illinois University.

Torts—Injuries to Family, Social and Trade Relations, 1979, 350 pages, by Wex S. Malone, Professor of Law Emeritus, Louisiana State University.

Trial Advocacy, 1979, 402 pages, by Paul B. Bergman, Adj. Professor of Law, University of California, Los Angeles.

Trial and Practice Skills, 1978, 346 pages, by Kenney F. Hegland, Professor of Law, University of Arizona.

Uniform Commercial Code, 1975, 507 pages, by Bradford Stone, Professor of Law, Detroit College of Law.

Uniform Probate Code, 1978, 425 pages, by Lawrence H. Averill, Jr., Professor of Law, University of Wyoming.

Welfare Law—Structure and Entitlement, 1979, 455 pages, by Arthur B. LaFrance, Professor of Law, University of Maine.

Wills and Trusts, 1979, 392 pages, by Robert L. Mennell, Professor of Law, Hamline University.

Hornbook Series
and
Basic Legal Texts
of
WEST PUBLISHING COMPANY

P.O. Box 3526
St. Paul, Minnesota 55165
March, 1980

Administrative Law, Davis' Text on, 3rd Ed., 1972, 617 pages, by Kenneth Culp Davis, Professor of Law, University of San Diego.

Agency, Seavey's Hornbook on, 1964, 329 pages, by Warren Seavey, Late Professor of Law, Harvard University.

Agency and Partnership, Reuschlein & Gregory's Hornbook on the Law of, 1979, 625 pages, by Harold Gill Reuschlein, Professor of Law, St. Mary's University and William A. Gregory, Professor of Law, Southern Illinois University.

Antitrust, Sullivan's Handbook of the Law of, 1977, 886 pages, by Lawrence A. Sullivan, Professor of Law, University of California, Berkeley.

Common Law Pleading, Koffler and Reppy's Hornbook on, 1969, 663 pages, by Joseph H. Koffler, Professor of Law, New York Law School and Alison Reppy, Late Dean and Professor of Law, New York Law School.

HORNBOOKS & BASIC TEXTS

Common Law Pleading, Shipman's Hornbook on, 3rd Ed., 1923, 644 pages, by Henry W. Ballantine, Late Professor of Law, University of California, Berkeley.

Conflict of Laws, Goodrich and Scoles' Hornbook on, 4th Ed., 1964, 483 pages, by Eugene F. Scoles, Professor of Law, University of Oregon.

Conflict of Laws, Ehrenzweig's Treatise on, 1962, 824 pages, by Albert A. Ehrenzweig, Late Professor of Law, University of California, Berkeley.

Constitutional Law, Nowak, Rotunda and Young's Hornbook on, 1978 with 1979 Pocket Part, 974 pages, by John E. Nowak, Professor of Law, University of Illinois, Ronald D. Rotunda, Professor of Law, University of Illinois, and J. Nelson Young, Professor of Law, University of Illinois.

Contracts, Calamari and Perillo's Hornbook on, 2nd Ed., 1977, 878 pages, by John D. Calamari, Professor of Law, Fordham University and Joseph M. Perillo, Professor of Law, Fordham University.

Contracts, Corbin's One Volume Student Ed., 1952, 1224 pages, by Arthur L. Corbin, Late Professor of Law, Yale University.

Contracts, Simpson's Hornbook on, 2nd Ed., 1965, 510 pages, by Laurence P. Simpson, Professor of Law Emeritus, New York University.

Corporations, Henn's Hornbook on, 2nd Ed., 1970, 956 pages, by Harry G. Henn, Professor of Law, Cornell University.

Criminal Law, LaFave and Scott's Hornbook on, 1972, 763 pages, by Wayne R. LaFave, Professor of Law, University of Illinois, and Austin Scott, Jr., Late Professor of Law, University of Colorado.

HORNBOOKS & BASIC TEXTS

Damages, McCormick's Hornbook on, 1935, 811 pages, by Charles T. McCormick, Late Dean and Professor of Law, University of Texas.

Domestic Relations, Clark's Hornbook on, 1968, 754 pages, by Homer H. Clark, Jr., Professor of Law, University of Colorado.

Environmental Law, Rodgers' Hornbook on, 1977, 956 pages, by William H. Rodgers, Jr., Professor of Law, University of Washington.

Equity, McClintock's Hornbook on, 2nd Ed., 1948, 643 pages, by Henry L. McClintock, Late Professor of Law, University of Minnesota.

Estate and Gift Taxes, Lowndes, Kramer and McCord's Hornbook on, 3rd Ed., 1974, 1099 pages, by Charles L. B. Lowndes, Late Professor of Law, Duke University, Robert Kramer, Professor of Law Emeritus, George Washington University, and John H. McCord, Professor of Law, University of Illinois.

Evidence, Lilly's Introduction to, 1978, 486 pages, by Graham C. Lilly, Professor of Law, University of Virginia.

Evidence, McCormick's Hornbook on, 2nd Ed., 1972 with 1978 Pocket Part, 938 pages, General Editor, Edward W. Cleary, Professor of Law Emeritus, Arizona State University.

Federal Courts, Wright's Hornbook on, 3rd Ed., 1976, 818 pages, including Federal Rules appendix, by Charles Alan Wright, Professor of Law, University of Texas.

Future Interests, Simes' Hornbook on, 2nd Ed., 1966, 355 pages, by Lewis M. Simes, Late Professor of Law, University of Michigan.

Income Taxation, Chommie's Hornbook on, 2nd Ed., 1973, 1051 pages, by John C. Chommie, Late Professor of Law, University of Miami.

Insurance, Keeton's Basic Text on, 1971, 712 pages, by Robert E. Keeton, former Professor of Law, Harvard University.

Insurance, Vance's Hornbook on, 3rd Ed., 1951, 1290 pages, by Buist M. Anderson, Counsel, Connecticut General Life Insurance Co.

Labor Law, Gorman's Basic Text on, 1976, 914 pages, by Robert A. Gorman, Professor of Law, University of Pennsylvania.

Law of the Poor, LaFrance, Schroeder, Bennett and Boyd's Hornbook on, 1973, 558 pages, by Arthur B. LaFrance, Professor of Law, University of Maine, Milton R. Schroeder, Professor of Law, Arizona State University, Robert W. Bennett, Professor of Law, Northwestern University and William E. Boyd, Professor of Law, University of Arizona.

Law Problems, Ballentine's 5th Ed., 1975, 767 pages, General Editor, William E. Burby, Professor of Law Emeritus, University of Southern California.

Legal Writing Style, Weihofen's, 2nd Ed., 1980, 332 pages, by Henry Weihofen, Professor of Law Emeritus, University of New Mexico.

New York Practice, Siegel's Hornbook on, 1978, with 1979–80 Pocket Part, 1011 pages, by David D. Siegel, Professor of Law, Albany Law School of Union University.

Oil and Gas, Hemingway's Hornbook on, 1971 with 1979 Pocket Part, 486 pages, by Richard W. Hemingway, Professor of Law, Texas Tech University.

Partnership, Crane and Bromberg's Hornbook on, 1968, 695 pages, by Alan R. Bromberg, Professor of Law, Southern Methodist University.

Property, Smith and Boyer's Survey of, 2nd Ed., 1971, 510 pages, by Chester H. Smith, Late Professor of Law, University of Arizona and Ralph E. Boyer, Professor of Law, University of Miami.

Real Estate Finance Law, Osborne, Nelson and Whitman's Hornbook on, (successor to Hornbook on Mortgages), 1979, 885 pages, by George E. Osborne, Late Professor of Law, Stanford University, Grant S. Nelson, Professor of Law, University of Missouri, Columbia and Dale A. Whitman, Professor of Law, University of Washington.

Real Property, Burby's Hornbook on, 3rd Ed., 1965, 490 pages, by William E. Burby, Professor of Law Emeritus, University of Southern California.

Real Property, Moynihan's Introduction to, 1962, 254 pages, by Cornelius J. Moynihan, Professor of Law, Suffolk University.

Remedies, Dobbs' Hornbook on, 1973, 1067 pages, by Dan B. Dobbs, Professor of Law, University of Arizona.

Sales, Nordstrom's Hornbook on, 1970, 600 pages, by Robert J. Nordstrom, former Professor of Law, Ohio State University.

Secured Transactions under the U.C.C., Henson's Hornbook on, 2nd Ed., 1979, with 1979 Pocket Part, 504 pages, by Ray D. Henson, Professor of Law, University of California, Hastings College of the Law.

Suretyship, Simpson's Hornbook on, 1950, 569 pages, by Laurence P. Simpson, Professor of Law Emeritus, New York University.

HORNBOOKS & BASIC TEXTS

Torts, Prosser's Hornbook on, 4th Ed., 1971, 1208 pages, by William L. Prosser, Late Dean and Professor of Law, University of California, Berkeley.

Trusts, Bogert's Hornbook on, 5th Ed., 1973, 726 pages, by George G. Bogert, Late Professor of Law, University of Chicago and George T. Bogert, Attorney, Chicago, Illinois.

Urban Planning and Land Development Control, Hagman's Hornbook on, 1971, 706 pages, by Donald G. Hagman, Professor of Law, University of California, Los Angeles.

Uniform Commercial Code, White and Summers' Hornbook on, 2nd ed., 1980, approx. 1,202 pages, by James J. White, Professor of Law, University of Michigan and Robert S. Summers, Professor of Law, Cornell University.

Wills, Atkinson's Hornbook on, 2nd Ed., 1953, 975 pages, by Thomas E. Atkinson, Late Professor of Law, New York University.

JURISDICTION IN A NUTSHELL

STATE AND FEDERAL

By

ALBERT A. EHRENZWEIG

Late Walter Perry Johnson Professor of Law, University of California, Berkeley

DAVID W. LOUISELL

Late Elizabeth Josselyn Boalt Professor of Law, University of California, Berkeley

GEOFFREY C. HAZARD, JR.

John A. Garver Professor of Law, Yale University

FOURTH EDITION

ST. PAUL, MINN.

WEST PUBLISHING CO.

1980

Printed in the United States of America

Library of Congress Cataloging in Publication Data

Ehrenzweig, Albert Armin.
Jurisdiction in a nutshell, State & Federal.

(Nutshell series)
1. Jurisdiction—United States. I. Louisell, David W., joint author. II. Hazard, Geoffrey C., joint author. III. Title.
KF8858.Z9E35 1980 347.73'12 80-312

ISBN 0-8299-2086-2

E. L. & H.Juris. 4th Ed.

TO OUR STUDENTS

Who, to Face the Future, must Master the Present and the Past

*

PREFACE TO THE FOURTH EDITION

This revision brings the previous edition up to date. The original format has been retained, while changes in the law are reflected in text revision and updated citations. Reference is also made to the Restatement Second of Judgments, particularly Tentative Draft No. 5, which reflects change in the law in a number of respects. Some additional topics have also been addressed. As before, the aim has been a concise synopsis of the law. Further reference can be made to such works as Louisell and Hazard, Pleading and Procedure (4th ed. 1979), James and Hazard, Civil Procedure (2d ed. 1977), and Wright, Law of Federal Courts (3d ed. 1976).

G. C. H. JR.

February, 1980

*

PREFACE TO THE FIRST EDITION

Like the law of jurisdiction itself, this little text grows out of conflict and tension—between the dogma of Pennoyer and the struggle for the forum conveniens, between the practicing lawyer's craving for assured results and the theorizing scholar's yearning for reform, between the sense of the past and the demands of the present, between the urge for symmetry and the hope of fairness. This text, moreover, is based on the conviction that the usual, regrettable but probably unavoidable, separation of federal jurisdiction from jurisdiction in general in the law school curriculum, should at least be counteracted by access to an inclusive text, however small.

We believe firmly in the discussion method of teaching, especially for first year lawmen who typically pursue jurisdiction in pleading and procedure courses, but also for second and third year students of federal jurisdiction and conflicts law. We may then fairly be asked: Why a supplemental text? Is not any attempt at simplification akin to heresy, something like giving students shotguns with which to shoot sitting ducks—even drugging the ducks beforehand? For justification, we plead the intricacy of the subject, the shortness of life and a possible mellowing—some would say softening—of our judgment. Many of us may now be prepared to believe that the diligent student who has ground his way through the cases in perplexity and wonder, perhaps has earned the right to know something of the perplexity and wonder of those who have gone before him—and what they have made of it all. As for the less than diligent student—neither this nor any other text will buoy him if he has not learned from the cases how to swim in the current.

The brevity at which we have aimed has induced us to limit citations to the most important cases and, for fuller documentation, by both case law and literature, to refer to our own work, principally, Ehrenzweig, Conflict of Laws (1962) (AAE), and Louisell & Hazard, Pleading and Procedure: State and Federal (1962) (L & H). Lest this appear presumptuous, we append a list of other selected texts.

A.A.E.
D.W.L.

Berkeley, California
January 1964

OUTLINE

OUTLINE

*

ABBREVIATIONS

AAE	Ehrenzweig, Treatise on the Conflict of Laws (1962)
GS	Goodrich and Scoles, Conflict of Laws (4th ed. 1964)
L	Leflar, American Conflicts Law (1968)
L & H	Louisell and Hazard, Pleading and Procedure: State and Federal (4th ed. 1979)
NS	Ehrenzweig, Conflicts in a Nutshell (3rd ed. 1973)
PIL	Ehrenzweig, Private International Law (vol. 1, 1967; vol. 2, 1973)
Recueil	Ehrenzweig, Specific Principles of Private Transnational Law, Hague Academy of International Law, Recueil des Cours 125 (1969) 170–370
Rest. Conf.	Restatement of the Law of Conflict of Laws (1934, Supp. 1954)
RS Conf.2d	Restatement Second, Conflict of Laws (1971)
RSJ	Restatement, Judgments (1943)
RS J.2d	Restatement Second, Judgments, Tent.Draft Nos. 1–6 (1973–1979)
W	Weintraub, Commentary on the Conflict of Laws (1971)

*

SELECTED TEXTS *

American Law Institute, Restatement of the Law of Judgments (1943)

——Restatement of the Law of Conflict of Laws (1934) (cited Rest., Conflicts)

——Restatement of the Law Second, Conflict of Laws (1971) (Rest.Conf.2d)

——Restatement, The Foreign Relations Law of the United States, Ch. 2 (Bases of Jurisdiction) (1965)

——Study of the Division of Jurisdiction between State and Federal Courts. Official Draft (1969)

——Restatement Second of Judgments (Tentative Drafts 1–6, 1973–1979) (Rest.J.2d)

Anton, PIL (1967) (Scotland)

Baxter, Essays on Private Law: Foreign Law and Judgments (1966)

Beale, The Conflict of Laws (1935) (3 vols.)

Blume, American Civil Procedure (1955)

Castel, Conflict of Laws (2d ed. 1968) (Canada)

Cavers, The Choice-of-Law Process (1965)

Cheshire and North, PIL (8th ed. 1970) (England)

---

* This list does not include the authors' works. See Prefaces. Nor does it include works on special topics or casebooks, collections of essays and symposia. For more complete bibliographies, see AAE XLI–LI; PIL I and II; Recueil; L & H.

Cowen, Federal Jurisdiction in Australia (1959)

Currie, Selected Essays on the Conflict of Laws (1963)

Dicey and Morris, Conflict of Laws (8th ed. 1967) (England)

Falconbridge, Essays on the Conflict of Laws (2d ed. 1954) (Canada)

Goodrich, Conflict of Laws (4th ed., Scoles 1964) (GS)

Graveson, The Conflict of Laws (5th ed. 1965) 6th ed. 1969) (England)

James & Hazard, Civil Procedure (2d ed. 1977)

Johnson, The Conflict of Laws (1933–1937) (Canada)

Leflar, American Conflicts Law (3d ed. 1977) (L)

Minor, Conflict of Laws (1901)

Moore, Federal Practice (since 1938, 2d ed. with supplements)

Morelli, Diritto processuale civile internazionale (2d ed. 1954) (Italy)

Morris, The Conflict of Laws (1971) (England)

Nussbaum, Principles of Private International Law (1943)

Nygh, Conflict of Laws in Australia (2d ed. 1971)

Parker, School of Foreign and Comparative Law, Bilateral Studies in Private International Law (ed. Nussbaum and Galston, since 1951)

Pigott, Foreign Judgments and Jurisdiction (1908–1910)

Rabel, The Conflict of Laws, A Comparative Study, 4 vols. (1950–1964)

Read, Recognition and Enforcement of Foreign Judgments (1951)

Riezler, Internationales Zivilprozessrecht (1949)

Stimson, Conflict of Criminal Laws (1936)

——Conflict of Laws (1963)

Story, Commentaries on the Conflict of Laws (1st ed. 1834, 8th ed. 1883)

Stumberg, Principles of Conflict of Laws (3d ed. 1963)

Szászy, International Civil Procedure: A Comparative Study (1967)

Weintraub, Commentary on the Conflict of Laws (1971) (W)

Westlake, A Treatise on Private International Law (1st ed. 1858, 5th ed. 1912) (England)

Wharton, Conflict of Laws (3d ed. 1905)

Wright, Federal Courts (2d ed. 1976)

*

TABLE OF CASES

A

TABLE OF CASES

B

TABLE OF CASES

C

TABLE OF CASES

D

E

G

H

I

J

K

L

M

N

O

P

R

S

T

TABLE OF CASES

W

Y

Z

JURISDICTION IN A NUTSHELL

STATE AND FEDERAL

INTRODUCTION

---

§ 1. Theory. A citizen of a foreign country briefly visits the United States. While here he is sued in a state court by an American. Although the cause of action is alleged to have grown out of business relations abroad, the state court gets good "jurisdiction" over the foreigner to render an "in personam" judgment if he was served with process within the state. A resident of Tennessee, while flying over Arkansas on a commercial flight, is served with a summons from an Arkansas federal court in a lawsuit for breach of contract. Here too the court gets good "personal jurisdiction" over the Tennessean because he was served "within" Arkansas. And Rule 4(f) of the Federal Rules of Civil Procedure (Fed.R.Civ.Proc.) provides for most suits in federal court that the summons may be served "anywhere within the territorial limits of the state in which the [federal] district court is held." But even if a defendant is "personally served" within a state, its courts often will not take "jurisdiction" if the case against him involves land lying in another state, or if the court considers itself "forum non conveniens." Why the great significance generally accorded to the mere fact of service "within" the forum state; and why the exceptions?

A lawyer sues his client for a fee. The client is not a resident of the lawyer's state. Since the client cannot be personally served within that state, the lawyer relies for "jurisdiction" on the client's ownership of land within that state. The client does not appear in the suit; the lawyer gets judgment by default; the sheriff sells the land to a purchaser at an execution sale. But the purchaser does not get good title and may have to return the land because the lawyer's judgment against his client was void. It was not good as a "personal" judgment because the client was not served within the state, and a state's power respecting personal judgments over non-residents has long depended on catching them within the state. But if the client had been a domiciliary of the state where the lawyer sued, even "constructive" service on him by publication or personal service without the state would have been enough to justify a personal judgment against him. His allegiance to the state would be enough to justify exercise of the state's "personal" jurisdiction over him, despite his absence. And if despite his non-residence, the client's land had been brought within the "jurisdiction" of the court by a writ of attachment issued promptly after commencement of the lawyer's suit, the judgment would have been a valid "quasi in rem" judgment with regard to the attached land, although it would not have adjudicated the claim as such and would therefore not have been entitled to full faith and credit in another state to the same extent as an "in personam" judgment. Using the same technique, a plaintiff who cannot get "personal jurisdiction" over a defendant in plaintiff's state because the defendant cannot be found therein and is not a citizen thereof, and who cannot seize property of the defendant within the state, may yet collect his claim there if he is lucky enough to find therein an obligor of the defendant. For then he may serve the obligor with garnishment or equivalent process, and obtain "quasi in rem" jurisdiction over the defendant to the extent of the obligation thus garnished or otherwise attached. It has even been held that a non-resident motorist's liability insurer is such an obligor.

Similarly, judgments jurisdictionally predicated only on the presence of the contested property within the judgment state—e. g., judgments condemning land or quieting title thereto or settling a trustee's accounts respecting personalty—are valid as "in rem" judgments, but do not bind named defendants "personally." And today the validity of such a judgment even "in rem" depends on fair notice of the lawsuit having been given to the defendant in compliance with the due process of law guaranteed by the Fourteenth Amendment of the United States Constitution. The "res" indispensable to "in rem" judgments may also be an intangible such as a debtor-creditor, or parental relationship. In such cases whether the "res" involved in the lawsuit is really within the state may itself be a problem. Are shares of corporate stock within a state because the certificates representing them are physicially in the state? Or are the shares present at the corporate domicile, or at the place where the corporation's assets are located? Answers vary with the different purposes of the question. Is the "res" of the parent-child relationship within a state because the child is lawfully domiciled there? Apparently "No" for purposes of an affirmative judicial declaration of parental status, but "Yes" for purposes of a judicial decree negating such status. Does the distinction make sense?

A steel tank manufactured in State A by one of its residents explodes on a public highway of State B, injuring plaintiffs and damaging their nearby home. May they sue the manufacturer in State B under its modern "long-arm" type statute which gives its courts jurisdiction where a defendant has "committed a tortious act within the state?" Would the defendant's argument that the tort, if any, was committed in State A where the tank was manufactured, and hence is beyond the statute's purview, be overcome if the statute also provided for jurisdiction over a defendant who "commits a tortious act without the state causing injury to person or property within the state?" And would a statute of the latter kind be constitutional without a requirement of some additional connection between the defendant and State B?

So far we have spoken chiefly of cases where the defendants are individual persons. But what of corporations—by which so much of America's business is carried on? Of course, the states which incorporate the corporation or explicitly authorize it to do business therein, can and do subject such corporations to "in personam" jurisdiction upon personal service on a designated official of the corporation. But often foreign corporations should in fairness be suable even if not explicitly authorized to do business in the forum state. Hence, the evolution of the idea that corporations doing business within a state are present there for purposes of "personal service" and therefore "in personam" jurisdiction; and hence the more modern notion that other "minimum contacts" with the state make it fair to exercise "personal jurisdiction" even without personal service. But why should an interstate railroad, whose defective freight car causes injury in a state where it solicits business, to a citizen of that state, be able to defeat "personal jurisdiction" in that state? Any why, when a Pennsylvania corporation is sued in New York for negligently causing the burning of plaintiff's warehouse in Virginia, does the court acknowledge "personal jurisdiction" over the corporation because it was qualified to do business in New York, yet refuse to exercise that jurisdiction?

Do these various results fit any common rationale? Are they pieces of a jig-saw puzzle? Or a mere hodge-podge of chips cast off from the block as judicial woodchoppers have hewn away? Is jurisdiction based on "physical power," as the great Justice Holmes said? Or is the power approach essentially a "myth"? When after months, or possibly even years, of litigation, a case is dismissed because the court in which it was commenced finds itself lacking or unwilling to take "jurisdiction," is the result logically inevitable? Economically wasteful and avoidable? Can we do better with these problems of jurisdiction than we do? Certainly one cannot intelligently contemplate such questions without knowing why we do what we do.

The student already must clearly perceive that the word "jurisdiction" covers a multitude of ideas. It is indeed a chameleonic word, a cloak of many colors. Many senses in which it is used in Anglo-American law will be discussed presently (§ 2). Even then we shall not have exhausted our topic by any means. A suit is begun in a municipal court for money damages; the defendant counterclaims for an injunction against the plaintiff. The counterclaim is dismissed because the court, as an inferior tribunal, has no "equitable jurisdiction." A state's district or circuit court, although one of "plenary jurisdiction," may have no jurisdiction to probate a will because the "probate jurisdiction" is conferred by the state's constitution on probate courts only. And there are the many situations in which courts, though "having" and being willing to "take" jurisdiction, are said to be precluded from exercising it "on jurisdictional grounds." This may occur for example where the parties lack procedural "capacity," or where the cause of action is barred by death or lapse of time, by prior adjudication or public policy. Finally, even when all these hurdles have been taken and judgment has been recovered, the court of another state may refuse its recognition because of its lack of what we may call interstate jurisdiction.

The problem is more complicated in the United States than elsewhere in the common law world because of our federal system. After perhaps years of litigation in a federal district court, an appellate federal court—perhaps the United States

Supreme Court—may throw the case out for want of "jurisdiction," thus leaving the parties exactly where they were when the suit was commenced—because, e. g., it appears that there was not complete diversity of citizenship between all plaintiffs and all defendants; or because the case is finally held not to have arisen "under the . . . laws . . . of the United States." Some of these problems of federal jurisdiction are sui generis and will be separately dealt with. In many places the Federal Rules of Civil Procedure are prominently discussed because they offer representative solutions among divergent state procedures and, having been substantially adopted by more than half of the states and being currently revised, may hold the clue to ultimate uniformity. For selected provisions from the New York Civil Practice Law and Rules 1966 (cited NYCPLR) and from Fed.R.Civ.Proc., see Appendices A and B.

The student of "jurisdiction" faces what appears to him as a jungle. He must face it with a stout heart and the finely honed machete of an incisive mind. Even so, there is no guarantee that he can make of this jungle a neat park. But he can hew his way to certain paths of understanding. And perhaps eventually he can help contribute to a conquest of the jungle, and promote a law of "jurisdiction" less jungle-like and more akin to an ordered woods. But before he can intelligently think about tomorrow he must master much terminology and know what is going on today and why. This implies some knowledge of yesterday. Oh, to relieve the reality of things from the tyranny of words!

§ 2–1. Practice—more theory. You wish to start a lawsuit for your client. The first formal step usually is to file a complaint. Your choice of the most appropriate court will depend on many factors including tactical ones such as the relative ease of enforcement of the hoped-for judgment, your preference for a state or a federal court assuming both are available, your respect for the "competing" judges, or your appraisal of the prospective jurors' caliber. But above all, you will have to know whether the court of your choice "has" jurisdiction and if it has, whether it will be willing and able to "take" or exercise it.

Often, though not always appropriately, the word "jurisdiction" is also used in meanings other than those discussed so far. Thus, it may loosely denote the *courts of a state* ("several jurisdictions have held . . .") or a *territory* ("service within the jurisdiction . . ."). Even more loosely, "legislative jurisdiction" purports to designate the state whose law is said to "govern". Most unhappily, some courts use jurisdiction as a synonym of a meritorious claim ("this court has jurisdiction to decide for the plaintiff in this case"). And we may even be told that "courts have no jurisdiction to change the language of a statute." Levell (Neb.1967).

For purposes of this discussion there are two relevant meanings of the term "jurisdiction." The first is "territorial jurisdiction." Rest.J.2d § 4. This refers to the authority of a state within the United States (or a nation within the world political community) to adjudicate a controversy in its courts. Generally speaking, a state has territorial jurisdiction if the persons involved in the litigation are present or domiciled in its territory or if the transaction in question has a substantial connection therein. The second meaning is "subject matter jurisdiction." Rest.J.2d § 14. This refers to the authority of a particular court to adjudicate a controversy of a particular kind. Thus, within the state of California the Superior Courts of that state have subject matter jurisdiction of suits in which the amount in controversy exceeds $15,000, while the Municipal Courts have subject matter jurisdiction of suits where the amount in controversy is that sum or less. "Subject matter jurisdiction" is sometimes referred to as "competence." Rest.J.2d § 14.

There are important conceptual and procedural differences between territorial and subject matter jurisdiction. Perhaps the most important difference is that territorial jurisdiction can be waived by a party's submitting to the court; subject matter jurisdiction cannot be waived, although a defect of subject matter jurisdiction does not necessarily render a judgment void. Thus, if a party makes an appearance in an action, no question of territorial jurisdiction can thereafter be raised; but an objection to subject matter jurisdiction can be raised, even as late as in an appeal from the judgment.

Jurisdiction in either of the foregoing senses should be contrasted with *venue*. Rest.J.2d § 7. Rules of venue are prescribed in each state, and for the federal district courts in the federal system. They specify the location where the action properly should be brought. For example, typical state venue rules permit an action to be brought in the county where one of the defendants resides. Hence, if defendant resides in X county, an action can be within the *subject matter* jurisdiction of the Superior Court and have its *venue* properly sited in the Superior Court for X County. Improper venue is waived by failure to object. See § 43 infra.

§ 2-2. Practice—realities. You will first make sure that the court of your tentative preference has jurisdiction over the subject matter. You will not begin a suit for damages for tort or breach of contract in a court which has only criminal or probate jurisdiction. And you will not claim $25,000 damages in a court which cannot render a judgment for more than $1,000, or seek an equitable remedy such as an injunction in a court which is explicitly prohibited from granting equitable relief. Usually, the constitution or statutes of your state will set forth the subject matter jurisdiction of the various courts, explicitly and clearly. Though sometimes even in this area difficulties may arise, for example, as to whether the relief sought is "equitable" within the meaning of a prohibition against equitable relief in a court of limited jurisdiction such as a municipal court; or whether a counterclaim may exceed the dollar limitation prescribed by the statute for an original claim. We will assume that your case is one appropriate for a trial court of general or so-called plenary jurisdiction, i. e., a court that has all the original jurisdiction not given explicitly to other courts and that has no dollar limitation on the amount of potential recovery, e. g., the California Superior Court, or the Minnesota District Court, the Michigan Circuit Court, or the New York Supreme Court.

We will also assume that you have selected the appropriate venue, which is normally not difficult. Thus, by explicit provision of statute, an appropriate venue for the typical tort or breach of contract suit is the county of residence of the defendant. The defendant can usually waive his right to a prescribed venue and will be deemed to have waived it if he does not seasonably insist upon it. But if he does insist upon it he can obtain either a dismissal of your lawsuit or at least its transfer to an appropriate venue.

Once you have established that the court of your tentative preference has jurisdiction over the subject matter and that you have chosen the proper venue, you may come to a problem of territorial jurisdiction if the defendant does not permanently reside in the state where you wish to sue. The problem is whether there is any way effectively to bring the defendant, or his property, before the court in such manner as to afford your client practical relief if you are able to establish a good cause of action. The territorial jurisdictional problem falls into two and sometimes into three parts: (1) whether your state's applicable statute, or other governing legal rule, purports to set forth a way to obtain jurisdiction over defendant or his property; and (2) if so, whether your state's prescribed way comports with the Due Process of Law clause of the Fourteenth Amendment to the United States Constitution. (3) If you expect to effectuate your judgment outside the state in which you originally obtain it, the additional question will arise whether the state of effectuation will be compelled by the Full Faith and Credit Clause of the Constitution to recognize your judgment or will at least be likely to do so on grounds of comity to the judgment state. The requirements of due process and full faith and credit are usually the same, so as to make the answers to the second and third question coincide. But a court's judgment may be within due process and yet not be entitled to full faith and credit in other states; and it may satisfy the requirements of both due process and full faith and credit and yet exceed the scope of the statute of its state.

Until very recently, your problem of "getting" jurisdiction, in the sense of inducing the court effectively to deal with the defendant or his property, would have differed according to whether your client's case is one involving a "personal" action or is related to his interests in a "res." That is, the important thing would have been whether you were depending on the court's "jurisdiction in personam" or its "jurisdiction in rem." In the first case traditional theory would have required you to secure the court's "power" over the defendant's person by proper service of process within the court's territory. In the latter case location of the "res" in the court's territory would have been deemed sufficient.

As we shall see the foregoing distinction has lost much of its practical and theoretical meaning. On the one hand, personal actions have become possible against absentees who for various reasons can in fairness be expected to defend themselves in the state where the suit is brought, for instance if they do business in that state. And on the other hand, it is now established that the presence of a defendant's property within the state is not necessarily a sufficient basis for seizing it as a way of enforcing the claim against him. Shaffer (U.S.1977).

Nevertheless, it remains necessary to start with the classical analysis since courts continue, and are likely to continue for some time, to arrive at their decisions with the help of traditional distinctions. What renders this classical analysis cumbersome is the fact that it must largely proceed in historical sequence. For courts, though their actual decisions are simple and predictable enough in terms of common sense reasoning, may at any time seek and find new law by using a seemingly obsolete precedent. Thus, in attempting to describe the present state of the law, we shall have to accept the customary distinctions, including those between jurisdiction in personam and jurisdiction in rem, and, in view of their divergent history, also between jurisdiction over individuals and corporations. And finally we shall have to incorporate in our scheme a hybrid concept formerly known under the term of quasi in rem jurisdiction and now called attachment jurisdiction. Rest.J.2d § 11.

"Terms such as in rem, quasi in rem, and in personam, seldom solve jurisdictional problems and are often misleading shorthand for the result." Thus wrote Chief Justice Traynor. Whealton (Cal.1967). See also Hazard, A General Theory of State Court Jurisdiction (1965 Sup.Ct.Rev. 241) and von Mehren and Trautman in their Harvard article (1966). Increasingly, the legal profession will develop a terminology more appropriate to norms of "interstate venue" than the historic language of "jurisdictional" limitations. § 4-15.

Beyond the problems of territorial jurisdiction, subject matter jurisdiction, and venue, is the problem of *notice*. At one time actual notice, through service of process, was required only in actions in personam. For actions in rem "constructive service" was held sufficient; "constructive service" meant published notice in a newspaper or posting a notice on property that had been seized. Under modern interpretation of the Due Process Clause, "constructive" service ordinarily is insufficient. Whether the action is in personam or in rem, or for attachment, means "reasonably calculated to give actual notice" must be used. Mullane (U.S.1950); Rest.J.2d § 5.

JURISDICTION IN PERSONAM

1. INDIVIDUALS

A. The Pennoyer Rule

§ 3–1. In 1878, the Supreme Court of the United States established the rule that a court may take personal jurisdiction over the defendant only and always if process was served on him personally within the state. Pennoyer v. Neff (U.S. 1877); W 86–88. By "process" is technically meant the summons, but the usual requirement for personal service is that a copy of the summons together with a copy of the complaint be left with defendant. Statutes may provide for such reasonable equivalents of personal service in this literal sense as the leaving of process at the place of the defendant's usual abode with an adult person resident there. See Nowell (C.A.5, 1967 Tex.). Fed.R.Civ.Proc. 4(d)(1). Such service is here referred to as "substituted" personal service in distinction from the "constructive" service. See § 2–2. But it should be remembered that some courts and writers often use these terms interchangeably.

§ 3–2. Personal service sufficient. The first facet of the Pennoyer Rule subjects to personal jurisdiction anybody personally served within the state, even if he is a mere transient and the case has no contact with the state in which he is "caught." This "transient rule" of personal jurisdiction is doubtful in origin and merit. 65 Yale L.J. 289 (1956); W 97; L 43. But it is clearly the law. Barrell v. Benjamin (Mass. 1819); MacLeod v. MacLeod (Me.1978). Certain *immunities*, to be sure, constitute exceptions from this rule. Infra § 28. But other exceptions have so far been urged unsuccessfully.

Hardships caused by the transient rule can be avoided by a recourse to the doctrine of *forum non conveniens* in the federal courts and in the courts of those states which have adopted it. § 17.

§ 3-3. Personal service required. The second facet of the Pennoyer Rule, the requirement of personal service within the state, on the other hand, has been long since modified by a series of leading cases in which various factors have been held constitutionally sufficient to give jurisdiction over absentee defendants by such means as personal service outside the state or by mail. But we cannot stress strongly enough that these cases are relevant only within the framework of the jurisdictional statute of your state.

Thus, process may be served outside of your state only if (1) your state statute authorizes such service in the type of case involved, *and* (2) the statute is itself valid under the limitations of the Due Process Clause. Today, generally speaking, the Due Process requirement is that the suit have some reasonable connection with the state in which it is brought. See § 4-13.

In some states the statute governing service of process simply incorporates the Due Process standard, so that only one question is posed in determining territorial jurisdiction: Does the state have a sufficient connection with—"minimum contacts" or some other basis—the suit. For such a statute see Cal.Code Civ.Proc. § 410.10. Other state statutes were construed to have that effect in Martin (Ala.1967); O'Hare (C.A.7, 1971 Ill.); Vemco Plating (Okla.1972); Duplan (D.C. S.C.1971); Lawson (E.D.Tenn.1971); Gurley (C.A.5, 1972 Tex.). Such jurisdictional statutes are usually held to be retroactive. Property Owners (N.H.1971); Cox (Colo.1966); Sussman (Pa.1971).

The great number of cases decided every year would render futile any attempt to establish general standards within this framework even for individual jurisdictions. No wonder that the American Law Institute had to state its "Principle Underlying Judicial Jurisdiction over Persons" simply, though unhelpfully, as requiring "a person's relationship to the state [which] is such as to make the exercise of such jurisdiction reasonable." Rest.Conf.2d §§ 24(1), 39.

B. Pennoyer Modified

(1) CONSENT

§ 4–1. Consent after accrual of a cause of action. Parties cannot confer on a court "subject matter jurisdiction", i. e. they cannot "enlarge the types of cases a court has been authorized to hear by the state." Owen Equip Co. v. Kroger (U.S.1978); Rougeron (N.Y.1966); McCray (Md.1972); Bryan (Tex.Civ.App.1972); Crafton (Com.Pa.1972); Rest.Conf.2d § 32 Comment b. But they can effectively consent to a court taking jurisdiction over their persons. Rest.Conf.2d § 32; Rest.J.2d § 13. A state may constitutionally permit cross-actions against a plaintiff upon service of process on his attorney by virtue of the plaintiff's submission to the jurisdiction he has invoked for his own claim, if the claim is related to the original action or if considerations of justice otherwise warrant subjecting plaintiff to the claim. Adam (U.S.1938); Rest.J.2d § 12.

§ 4–2. Appearance. The defendant's general appearance, i. e., an appearance lacking expression of a limiting intent, is equivalent to consent. Janson (N.H.1972); Rest.J.2d § 13. Earlier attempts by some states to deny opportunity to challenge territorial jurisdiction through a "special" appearance have been abandoned. See York (U.S.1890); W 166. Regarding the related problem of "limited appearance" in respect to attachment jurisdiction, see infra § 6–9.

Does an appearance imply consent also to an amendment of the original complaint? A leading court has so held regarding a $350,000 libel claim added to a $46,900 contract suit. Everitt (N.Y. 1958). But a limitation of this doctrine seems urgently required in view of the great liberality of the amending power in modern practice.

§ 4–3. Consent prior to accrual of cause of action. Parties to a contract may agree that any cause of action arising therefrom is to be subject to the jurisdiction of a specific court (prorogation). § 23. They may also to the same effect designate an agent to accept service of process in a particular state. National Equipment (U.S. 1964); Fed.Rule Civ.Proc. 4(d)(1); W 100–101; infra § 23. But the question, long controversial, whether the parties may validly confer a power of attorney to confess judgment (*cognovit* judgments) seems to tend towards a negative answer. The New York Court of Appeals has refused to enforce a Pennsylvania judgment of this type on the ground that it was not based on "judicial proceedings within the intendment of the full faith and credit clause and that the underlying warrants of attorney themselves violated due process because of their unlimited authority to enter judgment anywhere in the world." Atlas Credit (N.Y.1969); W 81–82, 101–102; infra § 36–2.

§ 4–4. Continuing jurisdiction. Once jurisdiction is acquired, it continues throughout the same litigation. Michigan Trust (U.S.1913). But "reasonable notice and reasonable opportunity to be heard must be given the party at each new step in the proceeding." Rest.Conf.2d § 26. See Griffin (U.S.1946). These rules are particularly important and, therefore, broadly interpreted in support and child custody cases. Blum (Ohio 1967); Varone (D.C.App.1972). Since litigation in such cases is often renewed over long periods, time limitations may be found necessary. Compare Sheffield (Va.1966) with Madsen (N.H. 1971); AAE § 27(3). And sister states are likely to claim concurrent jurisdiction. Grodziski (Minn.1967).

(2) FORUM BENEFITS AND ACTIVITIES ("LONG–ARM" STATUTES)

§ 4–5. Nonresident motorists. Jurisdiction has long been assumed over nonresident motorists who have caused an accident in the forum state. Such statutory jurisdiction was originally based on the presumption of the defendant's implied consent. Hess (U.S.1927); J. & H. § 12.14. Constructive service in such cases in usually prescribed upon a state officer. Other methods may be admitted (NYCPLR § 308) such as out-of-state service by mail. Dobkin (N.Y.1968). But the authorizing statute must prescribe a notification of the defendant which makes "it reasonably probable that he will receive actual notice." Wuchter (U.S.1928); Manley (Hawaii 1968); W 72–73. Such statutes have also been held to include nonresident owners who had consented to their car being taken into the forum state. Davis (C.A.4, 1961 N.C.). Concerning owners of *water craft*, see Philippine (C.A.5, 1964 La.). Many states permit constructive service also upon *administrators* of deceased motorists. Infra § 28–7.

§ 4–6. Domicile and residence. A "state which accords privileges and affords protection to [a person] and his property by virtue of his domicile may also exact reciprocal duties." Milliken (U.S.1940). It may, therefore, take jurisdiction over him if service is "reasonably calculated to give him actual notice" (id.) and, as always, if a statute expressly provides for such jurisdiction. Arakaki (Hawaii 1972); Duncan (N.H.1964). For this purpose "a domicile once established continues until it is superseded by a new domicile." Stucky (Neb.1971); generally, Rest.Conf.2d §§ 11–23. Residence is increasingly held to be equivalent to domicile for jurisdictional purposes, particularly in divorce cases (§ 8–2). Service by publication has been held constitutional against "a resident who hides himself" in the state. Gill (Minn.1967).

§ 4–7. Citizenship. Citizenship in a state of the Union is synonymous with domicile. In international litigation, the Supreme Court has held that the defendant's American citizenship is an adequate basis for serving a subpoena on him in France. Blackmer (U.S.1932). See also 28 U.S. C.A. §§ 1783, 1784 (1964).

§ 4–8. "Doing business." In 1935, the Supreme Court held the forum's regulatory power over an individual's forum activities implied also authority for its courts to assert territorial jurisdiction over him. Henry L. Doherty (U.S.1935). Today jurisdiction may be asserted "with respect to causes of action arising from the business done in the state" or where business "is so continuous and substantial as to make it reasonable for the state to exercise" jurisdiction. Rest.Conf.2d § 35; Uniform Interstate and International Procedure Act § 1.02 (1962). Doing-business statutes are often construed more narrowly with regard to individuals than with regard to corporations (§ 5–2). Zalevski (Pa.1966); Chrischilles (Iowa 1967); W 103–109.

§ 4–9. Ownership of property. We shall see that ownership of property can be the basis for either attachment (§ 6) or in-rem jurisdiction (§ 7). In addition, such ownership may support personal jurisdiction with regard to causes of actions arising from such property. But statutory construction has differed concerning the required relation between the cause of action and the property. Rivera (D.Mass.1971); W 129–130.

§ 4–10. Single acts in general. An increasing number of states, including New York, have followed the pioneer "long-arm" legislation of Illinois and Wisconsin and have based personal jurisdiction on specified single forum acts. These typically include the several stages of a contractual relation and of transacting business, on the one hand, and of the commission of a tort, on the other hand. W 109–129.

§ 4–11. (a) Contracts and "transaction" of business.

In Pennoyer v. Neff (U.S.1878), the Supreme Court had said that a state could exercise jurisdiction over nonresidents "making contracts enforceable" within the state. Taking a cue from this language many states adopted statutes providing that persons making local contracts could be subject to suit in the state, and that foreign corporations "doing business" within the state also could be subjected to jurisdiction. The "doing business" statutes were the forerunners of the latter "long arm" statutes. However, the "doing business" statutes were construed as requiring more than a specific act; rather, a continuous local connection was required. But if such a connection existed, it was generally held that the corporation was subject to suit not only on claims arising from the business done in the state but also on claims arising elsewhere. The theory was that the continuous connection that amounted to "doing business" was equivalent to presence, and under the Pennoyer Rule presence of the person was a basis for in personam jurisdiction regardless of whether the claim had any local connection.

The jurisdictional provisions referring to "making contracts" were given a narrower interpretation. It was generally held that jurisdiction existed only for claims arising out of the contract in question. Also, there was considerable hesitation in applying such statutes to individuals as distinct from corporations; Rest.Conf.2d § 36(2). The idea persisted for a long time that an individual could be sued only if he was personally served with process within the state. The "making contracts" provision has now found its way into the Illinois-type long-arm statute, i. e., statutes referring to various specific acts as a basis for jurisdiction.

The "doing business" provision is still retained in many statutes. They are generally interpreted to require the continuous connection that used to be regarded as indispensable for exercising jurisdiction. However, some courts give the "doing business" provisions a more modern interpretation. It has been said that "the test of whether business was transacted within the state must be applied in the context . . . of modern day commercial and personal accelerated relationships. The long arm statutes are comrades of the computer." O'Hare (C.A.7, 1971 Ill.); also Woodring (Kan.1968). The New York Court of Appeals, while excluding single out-of-state telephone calls [M. Katz & Son (N.Y. 1967)], had no difficulty in seeing a transaction of intrastate business in the participation by telephone in a New York auction. Parke-Bennet (N.Y.1970).

§ 4–12. (b) Torts. Besides nonresident motorist cases, torts concerning products liability are probably the most frequent. Since they almost exclusively concern corporations, they will be discussed in that context (§ 5–4). Regarding individuals, the only intimation we have had so far concerning the Supreme Court's attitude in this area, is an opinion by Justice Goldberg. Rosenblatt (S.Ct.1965). The Justice found "a very strong case for the assertion of 'long arm jurisdiction'," where the defendant was alleged to have "intentionally entered a State for the purpose of committing a tort therein." Earlier decisions concerning individuals would seem to favor a narrow interpretation of single-tort statutes. Fagan (Iowa, 1965) (neighbor moved after exploding a firecracker); Platt Corp. (N.Y.1966) (nonresident director's failure to attend forum meetings). But more recent decisions apply the same test of "reasonableness" to individuals as to corporations. Trustees of Sheppard Hospital v. Smith (R.I.1975). See also Kulko v. Superior Court (U.S.1978).

(3) GENERAL FORMULAS

§ 4–13. "Minimum contacts;" "fair play and substantial justice." All of these modifications of the Pennoyer Rule will ultimately have to be tested under the Supreme Court's guidelines. The fundamental formula remains that pronounced in 1945 in International Shoe (U.S.1945): As to both corporations and individuals a state may extend its Pennoyer jurisdiction to cases where it has "minimum contacts" and complies with "fair play and substantial justice." W 86–88. Within this formula, courts may apply such current statutory requirements as the accrual of a cause of action from domestic business (§ 5–3) or from regular business activities within the state, or even the newly fashionable search for their state's "manifest interest". Hines (Okla.1970). Availability of conditional dismissal by a forum non conveniens (§ 17) "may warrant sustaining service of process which otherwise might be vulnerable." Cooke (N.J.1973).

§ 4–14. "Purpose". But the clearest implementation of the Supreme Court's constitutional guideline is the requirement that the defendant have "purposefully [availed himself] of the privilege of conducting activities within the forum State, thus invoking benefits and protection of its laws." Hanson v. Denckla (U.S.1958); W 89–92. This requirement was reaffirmed in a tort case by Justice Goldberg's postulate "that the defendant must have taken voluntary action calculated to have an effect in the forum state." Rosenblatt (S.Ct.1965). It was reiterated in Kulko v. Superior Court (U.S.1978), where the Supreme Court rejected California's assertion of jurisdiction to enforce a support obligation against a parent who permitted his child to locate in California but who had not himself been in California.

(4) SELF-LIMITING STATE STATUTES— INTERSTATE VENUE?

§ 4–15. It should be remembered, however, that all these developments measure the state's maximum "long arm" authority. Some states have indicated an unwillingness to exert the fullest possible authority, thus showing concern for interests of nonresidents. Some states pursue this objective by incorporating a *forum non conveniens* provision in their jurisdictional statute. Cal.Code Civ.Pro. 410.30. Others do so by framing their "long arm" statutes so as not to reach to the fullest constitutionally permissible extent. Rest.J.2d § 7 Comment c.

2. CORPORATIONS

§ 5-1. History. The separate treatment of corporations in the law of jurisdiction is primarily due to an early and now receding hostility toward them. The hostility was expressed in the rule that a foreign corporation would not be recognized as a corporate entity in a sister state except upon the latter's grace and discretion. Bank of Augusta (U.S.1839). This premise that a foreign corporation could be excluded by a state led to the further proposition that a state could require a foreign corporation to "consent" to be sued locally as a condition of doing local business. Lafayette (U.S.1855). Thus, states could and did provide that a foreign corporation could not do local business until it registered with the state, and that if it failed to register it was deemed to appoint a state official as its agent for service of process. No such requirements could be imposed on individuals, who were protected by the Privileges and Immunities Clause. Later, of course, other theories were developed to sustain jurisdiction over individuals, beginning with the nonresident motorist statutes. See § 4-5. But by then (1927) the tradition of separate treatment for foreign corporations was long established.

A. "Doing-Business" Statutes

§ 5–2. Definition? The earlier statutes asserted jurisdiction over foreign corporations "doing business" in the state. "Doing business" was construed as requiring substantial local connection, such as an office, a resident employee, or the like. The comparison was with presence of an individual; hence, the question under "doing business" statutes was whether the corporation could be said to be "present." International Shoe (U.S.1945).

Other statutes, however, used the phrase "transacting business" in their foreign corporation statutes. Before the International Shoe decision, these statutes were generally interpreted in the same way as the "doing business" statutes. After International Shoe, however, states saw that a lesser connection was all that Due Process required. Hence, they interpreted "transacting business" statutes as satisfied by a single business connection, so long as the suit arose out of that connection.

The law today is probably as follows: If the cause of action arose out of a local activity by a foreign corporation, that activity will be held within the term "doing business" or "transacting business" in a state statute. If the cause of action did *not* arise out of local activity, however, the foreign corporation will not be subject to jurisdiction unless it has substantial continuing connection approximating local residence. In the latter situation the implicit comparison is to residence or domicile of an individual. The Supreme Court has held that a foreign corporation may be sued locally on a cause of action unrelated to the forum where (a) the corporation had its operating headquarters in the forum state and (b) there was no other place that the corporation could conveniently have been sued. Perkins (U.S.1952). Concerning the doing of business through subsidiaries, see infra § 28.

§ 5–3. Interstate commerce. The old "doing business" statutes went beyond subjecting foreign corporations to local jurisdiction. They also provided that a foreign corporation "doing business" locally could not bring an action in local courts unless it had registered as a foreign corporation. These provisions were held to violate the Commerce Clause of the Constitution as applied to corporations doing exclusively interstate business; such corporations were held to have a Constitutional right not only to do interstate business but also to enforce obligations arising out of such business.

Then came the expansion of the concept of "doing business" and "transacting business" for purposes of jurisdiction over foreign corporations.

The question inevitably arose whether the minimal concept of doing business for that purpose also meant that states could prevent foreign corporations with minimum contacts from suing. In Allenberg Cotton Co. (U.S.1974) the Supreme Court held that a foreign corporation entering contracts in interstate business with local persons could not be excluded from suing to enforce such contracts. Hence, a foreign corporation may be sued locally with only minimum contacts, but must have a substantial local presence before it can be required to register as a foreign corporation. Such presence was found in Eli Lilly & Co. (U.S.1961).

B. "Single-Act" Statutes

(1) IN GENERAL

§ 5–4. As against foreign corporations even more frequently than as to individuals (§§ 4–10, 11, 12), long-arm statutes have based jurisdiction on single acts (contracts or torts) within the forum state. W 109–129. Jurisdiction based on single *contract* statutes has long been upheld by state courts of last resort. McGee (U.S.1957); Byham (N.C.1965); 23 A.L.R.3d 537.

Single *tort* statutes are more problematic in view of the typical fortuity of the contact. W 113–125. They are phrased in terms of a "tortious act", of "negligent acts or omissions," of torts committed in the forum state "in whole or in part", or of acts "resulting in accrual of a tort action" in that state. Rest.Conf.2d §§ 49, 50. Typical for the problems of interpretation is a 1972 case in which a false statement intended to be relied on in the forum state and to cause injury to the plaintiff there, was held to constitute an "act" committed in the state of the plaintiff's residence. Murphy (C.A.1, 1972 Mass.). Cf. American Eutectic (C.A.2, 1971 N.Y.)

Similar problems concern tortious omissions. In New York "to treat an 'omission' as an 'act' in a particular place, one must be there to do or to omit the act." Platt (N.Y.1966). Cf. W 116, 134. But the interpretation of single-tort statutes has caused the greatest difficulty with regard to the foreign manufacturer's liability for products manufactured outside, but distributed or consumed within, the forum state.

(2) PRODUCTS LIABILITY

§ 5–5. Forum injury. Where the statute is satisfied by the commission in the forum state of a tort "*in whole or in part*," as for example in Iowa, Minnesota, Texas Vermont and West Virginia, or where the statute merely requires the causation of an "injury within the state" as in New York or Massachusetts, or where it is held to go to the constitutional limit as in New Hampshire, courts should be expected to have little choice but to affirm jurisdiction in cases in which the harm has occurred in the forum state. Coe (Ga.1973); Tice (Iowa, 1966); Engine Specialties (C.A.1, 1972 Mass.). But it is hardly enough to rationalize such holdings on the ground that "manufactured products are ordinarily designed for commercial sale in whatever markets may be found for them, without regard to state lines." Andersen (Iowa, 1965).

Instead, most courts use a *foreseeability* test. This may be done by statute, as in Connecticut, New York (combined with a "substantial-revenue" requirement, App. A), Maryland [Lamprecht (Md.1971)], and North Carolina, or by judicial legislation, Metal-Matic (Nev.1966), Jetco (C.A.5, 1973 Tex.), and Deveny (C.A.2, 1963 Vt.). Cf. Myers (Pa.1967); W 119–121. The foreseeability test is frequently and preferably combined with the "*purpose*" test of the Hanson case. § 4–14. Under a similar formula, the defendant must have "significantly entered the business life [of the forum state so that it may fairly be prevented from avoiding] the 'distasteful consequences' of suit." Engine Specialties (C.A.1, 1972 Mass.).

§ 5–6. Forum act. "Whole-or-in-part" and "injury" statutes are, of course, advantageous to the plaintiff. On the other hand, "*tortious* act" statutes seem to favor the defendant. Further implementing this policy, some states may, under such statutes, deny jurisdiction even to plaintiffs who were injured by a foreign product in the state of their residence. Most states, however, seem to favor the plaintiff in such cases, though often seeking to prevent hardship to the defendant by permitting it to claim non-foreseeability or noncompliance with the "purpose" test of Hanson (§§ 4–13, 5–5). Gray (Ill.1961); Sohn (Me. 1971); Deutsch (Wash.1972); Scanlan (D.Mont. 1972).

§ 5–7. New answers? A nationwide jurisdiction, limited by requirements of "fair play" to a forum conveniens (§ 4–16), may yet become the basis of a law of interstate venue (§ 4–15), with or without federal legislation. It was a products liability case in which the California law of jurisdiction was summarized to the effect that "once the threshold of sufficient activity by the defendant has been passed, the question of the propriety of subjecting the defendant to the jurisdiction of the forum involves both a consideration of fairness to the plaintiff and a determination of whether, from a standpoint of the logical and orderly distribution of interstate litigation, the forum state is what Ehrenzweig has termed a 'forum conveniens.'" Buckeye (Cal.1969) 899; also Roy (N.H. 1972). Another synthesis was by Justice Blackmun while a judge in the Eighth Circuit, Aftanase (8th Cir. 1965), as summarized in Hardrives, Inc. (Minn.1976). There are five factors: "quantity of contacts"; "nature and quality of contacts"; "the connection or relationship between the cause of action and the contacts"; "the state's interest in providing a forum"; and "convenience of the parties."

(3) LIBEL

§ 5-8. The difficulties under single-tort statutes in products-liability cases are compounded in cases involving libel committed through the means of mass communication such as newspapers, radio, or television. W 121–125. Here, the intangible character of, and the resulting difficulty in localizing, the harm caused to the plaintiff's reputation, could be made to support a virtually world-wide jurisdiction.

Some courts have tried to protect the defendant by various devices. They have resorted to a restrictive statutory interpretation, following the "purpose" test of Hanson (§ 4-14). Breckenridge (Miss.1965). Or they have adopted a novel "definite-interest" requirement said to be absent in suits between nonresidents. Curtis Publishing (C.A.5, 1966). Or they have found a constitutional need for particularly strong "minimum contacts," because "First Amendment considerations surrounding the law of libel require a greater showing of contact to satisfy the due process clause than is necessary in asserting jurisdiction over other types of tortious activity." New York Times, (C.A.5, 1966). See Margoles (D.C.D.C. 1971). Or they have assumed a general foreseeability test, sometimes taking into account the fairness of the potential applicability of forum law. Roy (N.H.1964). Or they have relied on the limiting effect of the Uniform Single Publication Act. Insull (N.D.Ill.1959). Finally, it has been intimated that, while broad statutory jurisdictions must be conceded at least in favor of resident plaintiffs, "the First Amendment could be regarded as giving forum non conveniens special dimensions and constitutional stature in actions for defamation against publishers and broadcasters." Buckley (C.A.2, 1967 Conn.). New York has specifically exempted actions "for defamation of character" from the reach of her long-arm statute. In Church of Scientology (9th Cir. 1978), it was said that the First Amendment does not impose special limitations on long arm jurisdiction in libel cases; however, in that case the court rejected jurisdiction in factual circumstances that would probably have sustained jurisdiction if some other tort had been involved.

(4) MULTI-PARTY LITIGATION

§ 5-9. Traditional territorial jurisdiction theory concerned itself solely with the connection between the state asserting jurisdiction and the particular defendant sought to be subjected to jurisdiction. This was true under both the *Pennoyer* approach and the "contacts" approach in *International Shoe.* However, in more recent years the emphasis on "convenience" has led to enlargement of the frame of reference in considering whether a particular defendant is subject to territorial jurisdiction. In this new frame of reference it also is relevant to consider whether *other* parties can be brought into the litigation in a specific state.

This concept was suggested in Buckeye Boiler (Cal.1969). There the court noted that California had an interest in hearing the action against the defendant Ohio corporation because a concurrent tortfeasor residing in California could be joined as a co-defendant in California but not Ohio. In a number of subsequent cases this concept has been expanded. Thus, jurisdiction has been sustained over a non-resident individual who had limited involvement in a local transaction but who was a necessary party to an adjudication between two other parties. Barer (Wash.App. 1978). Similarly, where a defendant sought to implead another person as a third-party defendant, territorial jurisdiction has been sustained over the third-party defendant partly by reference to the importance of resolving the three-way dispute in a single litigation. Fantis Foods (N.Y.App.Div.1978).

A more recent expansion of the concept is in class actions. It has been held that if some members of the plaintiff class are in the state and the defendant is subject to the state's territorial jurisdiction, a class action may be maintained in which the class includes claimants who live outside the state and who otherwise have no connection with the state. Shutts (Kan.1977); Schlosser (Wis.1978).

The concept can thus be restated as follows: The fact that a particular forum may be practically convenient for a litigation involving multiple parties is itself a factor in determining whether territorial jurisdiction may be asserted over those parties.

ATTACHMENT JURISDICTION

1. THE CONCEPT

§ 6-1. Terminology. Attachment jurisdiction is exercised when property within the state is seized in order to secure payment of a claim that is *unrelated* to the property. It is to be contrasted with in personam jurisdiction, where the basis of jurisdiction is a connection with the person who is sued; in attachment jurisdiction, the basis of jurisdiction is the existence of property owned by the defendant. Attachment jurisdiction is also to be contrasted with in rem jurisdiction, where the purpose of the action is to resolve conflicting claims to the property; in attachment jurisdiction both parties accept that the property is owned by defendant but plaintiff wants to expropriate it to pay his claim. Rest.J.2d §§ 9, 11.

Attachment jurisdiction used to be called, and is sometimes still called, "quasi in rem jurisdiction." But "quasi in rem" was also used to describe jurisdiction exercised to determine conflicting claims to property. In this usage, the term was used to contrast "true in rem" proceedings. To try to avoid confusion, the quasi in rem jurisdiction exercised to determine conflicting claims in property was called "quasi in rem jurisdiction type I"; attachment jurisdiction was called "quasi in rem jurisdiction type II." Rest.J. § 32. But this was still confusing. It is simpler to use the term attachment jurisdiction when plaintiff seeks to enforce a money claim unrelated to the property and seizes the property to secure payment of the claim. The term in rem jurisdiction is used to include all types of actions whose purpose is to adjudicate conflicting claims in the property in question. Rest.J.2d §§ 9, 11. Harris v. Balk (U.S. 1905); RS §§ 66–68; L § 45; W 142–143, 145–147.

§ 6–2. Origin. Attachment jurisdiction has been authorized by state statutes going back to colonial times. Usually the statutes were applied to permit attachment of local bank accounts or other assets having a more or less permanent location in the state. However, the Pennoyer Rule said that a state had authority to exercise jurisdiction over any property within its borders. This was interpreted to include a debt only temporarily in the state. In Harris v. Balk (U.S. 1905) the theory was stretched further: Harris, who owed money to Balk in North Carolina, went to Maryland. In Maryland, Epstein, with a claim against Balk, issued process by way of attachment against Harris. Thus, the debt from Harris to Balk was treated as "in" Maryland and seized there. Hence, the judgment in favor of Epstein expropriated Balk's claim. This procedure was held valid under the Pennoyer Rule.

§ 6-3. Fairness. The fairness of subjecting a person to suit where his property happens to be located has long been questioned. In some situations the forum seemed to be reasonably convenient. Thus, in Atkinson (Cal.1957), the debt seized in California was owed to a New Yorker, but the debt had arisen out of transactions in California involving the New Yorker and the California plaintiff. Hence, the claim could be said to have had "minimum contacts" with California. But in other situations, as in Harris v. Balk (U. S.1905), there was no such connection.

In Shaffer v. Heitner (U.S.1977) the Supreme Court held that the "minimum contacts" standard of fairness must be applied to attachment jurisdiction. Thus, ordinarily attachment jurisdiction may not be exercised unless the claim sued on has a reasonable connection to the forum, overruling Harris v. Balk. This requirement does not exclude use of attachment jurisdiction. For example in O'Connor (2d Cir. 1978), a New York plaintiff attached in New York an insurance policy in favor of defendant, to enforce a claim arising in Virginia. The court said the fact that plaintiff resided in New York was a sufficient connection for a suit to recover liability insurance against an injury occurring elsewhere. See also § 6-10. Also, in Carolina (N.D.Cal.1977) attachment was allowed in California of property owned by a French corporation in a suit by an American corporation over a claim arising out of an international transaction.

2. LIMITATIONS

§ 6-4. Debtor's exposure to double liability. The Supreme Court has said that "the failure on the part of the garnishee to give proper notice to his creditor of the levying of the attachment would be such a neglect of duty . . . as would prevent his availing himself of the judgment in the attachment suit as a bar to the suit of his creditor . . ." Harris v. Balk, supra.

A similar thought underlies the ruling that prejudgment garnishment proceedings without notification of the wage earner violate due process. Sniadach (U.S.1969). See also Fuentes (U.S. 1972).

§ 6–5. Multiple escheat. The Harris dictum foreshadowed the concern with the problem of double payment that faced the Supreme Court in an *escheat* case. Western Union (U.S.1961). In what has proved another important dictum, the Court announced that the exercise of jurisdiction on the basis of the presence of property may deprive its holder "of due process of law if he is compelled to relinquish it without assurance that he will not be held liable again in another jurisdiction or in a suit brought by a claimant who is not bound by the first judgment." Id. at 75. This dictum has since been interpreted by the Court as equivalent to the holding "that the Due Process Clause of the Fourteenth Amendment prevents more than one State from escheating a given item of property." And it has induced the Court, as a matter of "*ease of administration* and of equity," rather than of logic and jurisdiction [Texas v. New Jersey, (U.S.1965)], to hold each of 730 uncollected claims against a New Jersey corporation, "as to which a last known address of the person entitled thereto is shown on the books and records of defendant Sun Oil Company, [to be] subject to escheat or custodial taking only by the State of that last known address." Texas v. New Jersey (380 U.S.1965). In thus holding the Court rejected the theories advanced by four other states, based on the local origin of the debts, the place of defendant's incorporation, its principal business office, and the most significant contacts. In 1972, the Court added that, if no address is contained in the records or if the creditor's state has no escheat law, the right to escheat "shall be with the domiciliary state of the debtor." Pennsylvania (U.S.1972). In a novel use of the "ease-of-administration" technique, the situs of a taxpayer's property in the cash surrender value of his insurance policies has been found to be at the taxpayer's residence rather than at the physical location of the policies. Bankers Trust Co. (N.Y.1967).

The Western Union dictum can be said to indicate that the exercise of quasi-in-rem jurisdiction would violate due process where double liability could result from a judgment by the court of a foreign country which does not owe full faith and credit to a judgment based on such American jurisdiction. This assumption is reaffirmed by a dictum in First Nat'l City Bank (U.S.1965). Cf. Rest.Conf.2d § 68, Comment c.

§ 6–6. The race of diligence. The situs of intangibles is always fictitious. Several states, including those of the debtor's or creditor's presence or residence, or that of the location of a representative document may claim such a situs. Thus, a number of states could engage in a "race of diligence" so as to obtain the full faith and credit due the first judgment. See Great Falls Transfer (C.A.10, 1965 Wyo.). The Restatement's test of "reasonableness" merely restates the problem. RS § 65.

To limit the race, courts may insist on the situs within the state of "some physical property, or some debt . . . which is definite or capable of being made definite without contingencies, . . . which can be seized and appropriated," to the exclusion of a "mere expectancy." Camp (Ga.1965) (group annuity contract). See also Housley (Utah 1967); Cheff (Del.1967) (share of residuary legatee in specific assets); U.S. Industries (D.Del.1972). The impossibility of drawing a clear-cut distinction between "definite" claims and others to "conditional" to serve as the basis of quasi-in-rem jurisdiction is well illustrated in First Nat'l City Bank (U.S.1965) (dissent). Here the Government asserted such jurisdiction in New York over a Uruguay debtor by virtue of his conditional right to recover damages from a New York bank in case of its wrongful refusal of a demand for payment in Montevideo.

§ 6-7. Underlying cause of action. As a matter of Constitutional law, any kind of claim can be enforced by attachment jurisdiction. State statutes, however, have imposed limitations on the claims that may be so enforced. Thus, Pennsylvania permits "foreign attachments" only in "actions ex delicto for a tort committed within this Commonwealth." But Rule 1252 of the Pennsylvania Rules of Civil Procedure which purports to exclude attachment where the acts "were committed outside the Commonwealth," has been held not to prohibit attachment of foreign assets within Pennsylvania in actions based on injuries in Pennsylvania caused by out-of-state manufacturers. Wilk (Pa.1966).

§ 6–8. Stay. Sometimes "the court should stay further proceedings until controverted matters are litigated in the appropriate forum". Fitch (Me.1966); Carolina (N.D.Cal.1977) (stay to allow arbitration).

§ 6–9. "Limited" appearance. The general effect of appearance on jurisdiction has been discussed earlier. § 4–2. When attachment jurisdiction is exercised may the defendant appear to defend on the merits but so limit his appearance that the judgment may not exceed the property attached? Such an appearance, if allowed, is called a "limited" appearance. Or does such an appearance necessarily constitute a general one because it is on the merits, so that the judgment may be in personam for the full amount of plaintiff's claim? The classic authority for the limited appearance is Cheshire Nat'l Bank (Mass.1916); contra, Anderson (D.C.Neb.1953). See Hansen (Wis.1971); W 143–144. Legislative trends toward abandonment of limited appearance, e. g. NYCPLR 320; Minn.R.Civ.Proc. 4.04(2) are countervailed by judicial adherence to the doctrine. Dry Clime (C.A.5, 1968 Miss.); see 4 Wright & Miller, Federal Practice and Procedure § 1123. Perhaps ultimately it will be held that whether or not the limited appearance is justified depends on whether plaintiff's selection of a forum was reasonable. Under this approach, only if plaintiff selected an unreasonable forum—and seizure of an evasive debtor's assets is normally justified wherever they can be found—should defendant be allowed a limited appearance. Where plaintiff has acted reasonably in choosing a forum, a defense on the merits normally should constitute a general appearance. See Rest.Conf. 2d § 75, Comment d; Rest.J.2d § 11, Comment g.

The Federal Rules of Civil Procedure, without directly confronting the problem of limited appearances in federal court, take care to avoid indirect sanctions against such appearances. Fed. R.Civ.Proc. 13(a) provides that a counterclaim even if otherwise compulsory, need not be stated by the pleader if the opposing party brought his suit by attachment or other process by which the court did not acquire in personam jurisdiction, and the pleader states no other cause of action.

This amendment accompanied the amendment to Fed.R.Civ.Proc. 4(e) which permitted federal district courts for the first time to exercise original quasi-in-rem jurisdiction. See § 54.

3. EXPANSION

§ 6–10. The "Seider doctrine." A New York resident sued a citizen of Connecticut in New York upon attachment of the latter's liability policy issued by a Pennsylvania insurer doing business and maintaining an office in New York. The New York Court of Appeals upheld the action, treating the policy as a "debt" under the Harris doctrine. § 6–2; Simpson (N.Y.1967), following Seider (N.Y.1966). This practice which in effect creates a direct action against the insurer (§ 35–2), has been held constitutionally proper. Minichiello (C.A.2, 1969 N.Y.). But it has been rejected in many states. De Rentiis (R.I.1969); Howard (S.C.1970); Housley (Utah 1967); Javorek (Cal.1976). And it has been held that the doctrine cannot be applied in an action which is "by nonresidents against other nonresidents who have no contacts with [the forum], and arises out of an occurrence in another state." Farrell (C.A.2, 1969 N.Y.). So long as the action is by a locally resident plaintiff, the "Seider" attachment action is held to be compatible with Shaffer v. Heitner (U.S.1977). O'Connor (2d Cir. 1978).

JURISDICTION IN REM

§ 7–1. The res. A state has authority to adjudicate claims of interest in property situated within the state. Rest.J.2d § 9; Rest.Conf.2d § 59. Under the Pennoyer Rule in rem jurisdiction was justified on the ground that the state necessarily had power over all things within its borders. Under the modern "minimum contacts" concept, in rem jurisdiction is justified on the ground that the presence of the property is itself an "affiliating circumstance" that makes exercise of jurisdiction reasonable. Atkinson (Cal.1957). However, under the "minimum contacts" standard, in some circumstances a state might not properly exercise jurisdiction to determine claims to property within its borders. For example, if property were forcibly and temporarily removed from the state where it was usually kept, the state where it was taken might determine its immediate proper custodian but not adjudicate ownership claims in it.

Property concerning which in rem jurisdiction may be exercised includes tangible property, both realty and chattels. It also includes intangibles such as shares of stock and bank accounts. However, with regard to intangibles difficult problems can arise in determining "situs." See § 6–5.

§ 7-2. Types of in rem jurisdiction. Formerly, in rem jurisdiction was subclassified into three types. The first was the "true" in rem proceeding. This was one in which the court undertook to adjudicate all claims of all persons to the property. Examples include the admiralty libel in rem, actions to quiet title against all claimants, and proceedings to settle a decedent's estate. The second was "quasi in rem type I." This was exactly like a "true" in rem proceeding, in that it undertook to adjudicate claims in the property, except that the adjudication concerned only the claims of certain specified persons. The third subclassification was "quasi in rem type II," which is now called attachment jurisdiction. See § 6-1.

This three-way classification was confusing. Attachment jurisdiction has no connection with in rem jurisdiction except for depending on the fact that locally situated property is involved; attachment jurisdiction is really a collection device. Furthermore, there is only an elusive distinction between "true" in rem actions and actions that are "quasi in rem type I." The only distinction is whether the proceeding undertakes to bind "all the world" or only certain named persons. This distinction in turn depends on what kind of notice is given of the proceeding. If notice is given only to certain specified persons, then only their claims are determined. If notice is given to all potential claimants, then all potential claimants are bound. Rest.J.2d § 9, Comment b, § 5, Comment g.

§ 7-3. The forum. "Proceedings in rem to determine the title to land must necessarily be brought in the State within whose borders the land is situated, and whose courts and officers alone can put the party in possession." Huntington (U.S.1892); Rest.Conf.2d § 59. Concerning intangibles there is difficulty of ascertaining the situs (§ 6-6). About all that can be said is that the situs of an intangible will be deemed to be in a state with which the intangible has a reasonable connection. Rest.Conf.2d § 65.

Title to property, whether tangible or intangible, can be determined in an action other than an in rem action. Thus, if an in personam action is brought for specific performance of a contract for sale of property, and judgment is given for plaintiff, the decree in effect transfers title. Such an in personam judgment may be entitled to recognition in the state where the property is located. The older cases regarded that as an impossibility for it would mean that one state could determine title to property in another state. Fall (U.S. 1909). But modern decisions uphold the validity of such a decree. Higginbotham (N.J.1966); Varone (7th Cir. 1966).

§ 7–4. Service of process. It was formerly held that in in rem actions a court may acquire jurisdiction as to nonresidents by mere *constructive service* of process. Arndt (U.S.1890). This rule was rationalized under the "caretaker theory" under which "property is always in possession of its owner" [Pennoyer v. Neff (U.S.1877) 727], so that owners usually can keep informed "of what concerns or may concern their real estate" [Ballard (U.S.1907) 269] and other property. But with increasing interstate migration and commercial intercourse this argument has lost much of its force. Much of what seemed reasonable notification at the time when constructive service was first accepted has long since become a "mere gesture", particularly when we are dealing with intangibles whose situs is always fictitious. Consequently, the Supreme Court declared unconstitutional as violating Due Process a New York statute which prescribed newspaper publication as the only required form of notice even as to known and reachable nonresidents. Mullane (U.S.1950) (judicial settlement of trust accounts). W 74–75. This rule has since been applied to proceedings for the condemnation of land. Walker (U.S.1956); Schroeder 1 (U.S.1962); W. 78. Many states have enacted legislation providing for mail or personal service outside the state in actions in rem. For purposes of notice, such proceedings are indistinguishable from proceedings in personam. Robinson (U.S.1972) (forfeiture of vehicle). See also Laz (Ariz.1964) (quiet title action); Fritz (Ind.1969) (sewer assessment); Rest.Conf.2d § 57. It is now settled that, whether the proceeding is in rem or in personam or for attachment, notice must be given "in a manner that actually notifies the person being addressed or someone who can adequately represent him, or has a reasonable certainty of resulting in such notice." Rest.J.2d § 5(1)(b).

DOMESTIC RELATIONS

§ 8–1. In most litigated cases a court will merely "declare" the existence or nonexistence of a legal relation as of the time it is alleged to have been created (ex tunc). In a divorce or adoption case, on the other hand, the court is asked "constitutively," as of now (ex nunc), to transform or create a new relation. In such cases a court may be reluctant to apply any law other than its own even when dealing with foreign citizens or foreign facts. Partly on that ground, American courts, in contrast to those of civil-law countries, have almost always applied their own law regarding grounds of divorce or the parties' capacities in adoption cases. Once the court has made this choice, it will ordinarily not be satisfied with personal jurisdiction which can affect mere transients (§ 3–2), and will take jurisdiction only if the "res" is situated within its territory. Hence, the basic rule that in adjudications of status, the status must be "present."

1. DIVORCE

A. Validity

§ 8–2. The domicile requirement. Since jurisdiction in divorce cases is based on the situs of the res of the marriage, the place of the spouses' *matrimonial* domicile would be the most obvious choice. This domicile was, indeed, the classical basis of jurisdiction. However, greatly varying degrees in the ease with which the several states have been willing to dissolve the marriage bond have often induced spouses to seek divorce outside the state of their common domicile. And most states have been increasingly inclined to recognize such "migratory" divorces by gradually extending their conceptions of the situs of the marriage as the basis of in rem jurisdiction. First it was the state of the *husband's* separate domicile [Atherton (U.S.1901)], later an *"innocent" spouse's* state of refuge [Haddock (U.S. 1906)] that claimed and were conceded such jurisdiction. And finally any divorce obtained at *either spouse's* "bona fide domicile" has come to be held to be entitled to interstate recognition. Williams v. North Carolina (U.S.1942) (Williams I); Rest.Conf.2d §§ 21, 71.

§ 8-3. Non-domiciliary divorces. Some states will grant a "quickie" divorce on colorable allegations that the plaintiff is a bona fide domiciliary. Usually no more is required than a minimum period of residence and a declaration of intention to remain in the state. Whether or not such divorces are entitled to full faith and credit in sister states is a complex problem of conflict of laws. AAE §§ 74-81; infra § 37. That such divorces are valid in the rendering state has never been decided by the United States Supreme Court. See Granville-Smith (U.S.1955); a dictum in Williams v. North Carolina (II) (U.S.1945), 229 suggests the affirmative. Alton (C.A.3, 1953 Vir.Isl.). Several state courts of highest resort have upheld statutes establishing *mere residence* for a specified period as a sufficient basis for divorce. Sachs (Ala.1965); Wheat (Ark.1958); Whitehead (Hawaii, 1972). Sometimes the statute in question is limited to military personnel. Lauterbach (Alaska, 1964); Wallace (N.M.1958); Wood (Tex.1959). In Sosna (U.S.1975), the Supreme Court sustained a state statute requiring one-year residency as a condition of obtaining a divorce. The Court observed that jurisdiction for divorce depends on domicile and that residency for a specified substantial period is strong evidence of domicile.

As a matter of state law, therefore, domicile is universally required as a basis for divorce jurisdiction. Some states have insubstantial tests of domicile, however, and thus can grant "quickie" divorces. But the frequency of such divorces has rapidly declined now that New York and other states have relaxed the grounds upon which they will grant divorce; ordinarily it is no longer necessary for New Yorkers to go to Nevada to get divorced.

B. Support

§ 9–1. Divisible divorce. An ex parte Nevada divorce decree has been held to be "divisible"—i. e., effective in New York "as it affects marital status and . . . ineffective on the issue of alimony." Estin (U.S.1948). Full faith and credit is not due, therefore, to any sister state judgment insofar as it purports to terminate a forum alimony decree in the absence of personal jurisdiction. Owen (Mich.1973). Yet any state remains free nevertheless to endow such a judgment with terminating effect. These principles apply also to *post-divorce* alimony. Thus it was held that "since the wife was not subject to its jurisdiction, the Nevada divorce court had no power to extinguish any right which [she] had under the law of New York to financial support from her husband." Vanderbilt (U.S.1957); Rest.Conf.2d § 74, Comment c. Migratory post-divorce alimony suits have been precluded in those states which require pre-divorce domicile for such suits. Loeb (N.Y.1958); infra § 37–6. Cf. Rheaume (R.I.1970).

§ 9–2. Uniform Act. Due to the requirement of personal jurisdiction, the deserting provider may be able to escape his obligation. The Uniform Reciprocal Enforcement of Support Act (1950, 1952, 1958), "Revised" (1968), now in effect in all states except New York and Iowa (with similar statutes), seeks to frustrate desertions. It enables the plaintiff to reach the provider with out-of-state process by filing a complaint in the plaintiff's "initiating" state. This complaint will be forwarded to the defendant's "responding" state which, exercising personal jurisdiction, will order and compel him to furnish support. AAE § 82; infra § 38. It is also increasingly recognized that the deserting provider remains subject to the personal jurisdiction of the dependent's state, since the cause of action had arisen in that state. Soule (Cal.App.1961). See Smith (Cal.1955). Such extended jurisdiction has been held entitled to full faith and credit. Mizner (Nev.1968).

These and other difficulties could be resolved by the universal adoption of the *registration* procedure provided in the 1968 "Revised" version of the Act. Brockelbank and Infausto, Interstate Enforcement of Support Decrees (2d ed. 1971) ch. IV.

2. ANNULMENT

§ 10. Three types of annulment must be distinguished: (1) those which are merely "declaratory" of the fact of nullity; and those which are "constitutive" because they create new legal relations by (2) either invalidating a marriage ex tunc (as either void or voidable); or (3) by dissolving the marriage ex nunc like a divorce. In suits for constitutive annulment, courts are more likely to take jurisdiction if their state refuses to grant a divorce on the facts pleaded by the defendant. AAE § 90.

In a few states, by virtue of statute or judicial practice, based on analogy to divorce cases, Rest. Conf.2d § 76(1), jurisdiction for annulment is satisfied by a plaintiff "domiciled" in the forum. Perlstein (Conn.1964); Singh (N.Y.Sup.1971). Most states have adopted what is in effect a theory of a "personal jurisdiction in rem". They require, in addition to personal service or consent, the compliance with a statutory or judicial provision relating to the location of the "res" of the marriage. This requirement may in effect limit jurisdiction to the place of celebration or to the place of at least the plaintiff's domicile. Foster (S.C.1964); Rest.Conf.2d § 76(b); AAE § 91.

3. ADOPTION

§ 11. Statutes usually confer jurisdiction upon courts of the adopter's domicile or residence and require the child to be within the court's territory. This jurisdiction could be classified as one in rem were it not for the fact that, in addition to the consent of the adoptive parents, of the child, and sometimes of the adoption agency, the consent of the adoptee's living natural parents may be required unless they have forfeited that right. Smith (Ga.1968). Service by publication is apparently insufficient without actual notice to such parents and their opportunity to be heard. Moreover, personal jurisdiction over such parents may be always required if jurisdiction is exercised over a child who is domiciled outside the forum state. It would seem desirable for the courts to discard the unsatisfactory dichotomy of jurisdiction in rem and in personam and, within their statutory authority, to approve adoptions whenever this seems proper for the welfare of the child, provided the rights of his natural parents have been safeguarded in the most effective manner. AAE § 26(5); Rest.Conf.2d § 78; infra § 40.

The Supreme Court has invalidated an adoption decree that was based in part on the Juvenile Court's assumption that the natural father had forfeited his right to consent by his failure to support the child. The Court found a violation of due process in that "no notice of any kind" had been given to the father of the filing of pendency of the petition. The Court's reliance on both the in-rem case of Mullane (§ 7) and the in-personam requirement of May (§ 14) perhaps points in the direction of the solution here suggested. Armstrong (U.S.1965); W 75.

4. PATERNITY

§ 12. Jurisdiction. Originally a remedy serving the *punishment* of the father or the prevention of a *public charge* by recoupment from him by the parish, the paternity suit has come to be primarily concerned with the *financial protection* of the child. This fact may account for the tendency to base such suits on personal jurisdiction over the alleged father in analogy to suits for support (§ 9). Hartford (Cal.1956). But this practice, while exposing the defendant to being "caught" as a transient, also may offer him refuge in states far removed from the child's residence. On the other hand, a theory of jurisdiction in rem with its greater latitude of notice and hearing would fail to offer sufficient protection to an innocent defendant. Perhaps the ultimate answer will be found in a personal jurisdiction which, on the one hand, would, for the protection of the plaintiff, be satisfied by service in the state of the alleged conception (§ 7), and, on the other hand, for the protection of the defendant, be limited by discretionary dismissal under the doctrine of forum non conveniens (§ 22).

5. CHILDREN'S CUSTODY

§ 13–1. In general. Jurisdiction to determine custody was originally governed by the principle of in rem jurisdiction. Sometimes the child was regarded as the *res*, sometimes the marital or parental relationship in which the child was situated, and sometimes the child's custody itself. The in rem concept of custody led to the proposition that a court could adjudicate custody against a nonresident parent without jurisdiction over the parent, and even without notice to the parent. The Supreme Court intervened under Due Process. Unfortunately it did not directly attack the notice problem, for example, by holding that a nonresident parent is entitled to notice whatever the theory of jurisdiction. Instead, it adopted the rule that custody determinations are binding only if the parent affected is subject to the court's personal jurisdiction. May (U.S.1953). This meant that if the child and the mother were in State X, and the father in State Y, no state could enter a custody decree that was effective against both parents. As a consequence custody decrees were often very unstable, and there was strong incentive for parental kidnapping.

In recent years the states have undertaken to overcome this difficulty. On one hand, they are more ready to accept jurisdiction without regard to domicile of the child or other requirements. On the other hand, once some court has assumed jurisdiction to award custody others will generally refrain from becoming involved if the original court retains jurisdiction. Under this theory, courts may assume or decline jurisdiction over domestic and foreign children, of domestic and foreign parents, without regard to earlier decrees of other courts and ignoring obsolete formulas, whenever the welfare of the child so requires [Hawkins (Ore.1972)] and the rights of both parents, including those of the natural father [Stanley (U.S.1972)], have been fairly protected. Cannon (S.C.1973); W 131–133, 194–196; infra § 39.

§ 13–2. Uniform Act. The Uniform Child Custody Jurisdiction Act 1968 seeks to "promote and expand the exchange of information and other forms of mutual assistance between the courts . . . concerned with the same child; and to make uniform the law of those states which enact it." § 1(a) (8–9). This is to be achieved (1) by the curtailment of simultaneous proceedings in different states (§ 6) which claim jurisdiction, be it in the state of the child's "home" or his presence; (2) by the registry of sister state decrees (§

16); and (3) by general assistance to sister state courts (§ 20). For other statutory formulas, e. g., Karol (Md.App.1971).

DECEDENTS' ESTATES

§ 14–1. Like much of the jurisdiction in cases concerning domestic relations, that governing the administration of decedents' estates defies classification as being either in personam or in rem. Thus, the decree of a foreign court to which all parties were subject, has been considered as having complied with the requirements of both types of jurisdiction. Staley (Md.1947). But cf. O'Brien (R.I.1966); Brewster (Conn.1964). See also Suffolk (Ill.1964). It is this hybrid character of jurisdiction in this area that also accounts for the competition in jurisdictional bases between the decedent's domicile and the situs of his assets in matters of probate. L § 201. See also Uniform Probate of Foreign Wills Act, 8 ULA 593 (1972).

§ 14–2. Domicile. In most states, probate or intestate administration will be opened in the proper court of the decedent's domicile. Rest. Conf.2d §§ 314(a), 315. That court's jurisdiction is generally considered primary as against any ancillary jurisdiction that might be assumed by courts over assets located within their territories. Rest.Conf.2d § 314(b). Whether the court of the domicile may extend its jurisdiction over foreign assets is not clear. Occasionally such extension has been considered a violation of due process. De Lano's Estate (Kan.1957). But the principal question in such cases is whether a domiciliary decree will be recognized in other states.

This question is unsettled. This much is clear, however, that *land* will always be dealt with independently by the court of the situs. Clarke (U.S.1900). And neither as to land nor as to personalty is the forum of the situs prejudged by another court's finding of domicile, at least as to any party not estopped from denying such finding by participation in the prior proceedings. Riley (U.S.1942); Rest.Conf.2d § 317(4). As to *personalty*, situs courts will occasionally extend full faith and credit to a sister state decree based on personal jurisdiction over the parties. Morgan Guaranty (N.Y.1971). And even when they refuse to do so, they may, except in international cases [Heller-Baghero (N.Y.1970)], in effect give recognition to domiciliary findings by applying the law of the domicile. Rest.Conf.2d § 317(1); Uniform Probate Code, 8 ULA (1972) § 3-408; AAE § 52. For a case illustrating the possibility of a "race of diligence" between federal and state courts, see Morell (Pa.1967).

§ 14-3. Situs. Courts of the situs of the property may take primary jurisdiction. Sherrill

(Ariz.1962). This will most frequently occur in international cases. Montgomery (C.A.D.C. 1966). Personal property is sufficient. Intangibles may, for this purpose, be localized at the "business situs"; where personal jurisdiction over a debtor or his property has been obtained; or, generally, where the exercise of jurisdiction appears "reasonable". GS §§ 181–184.

JURISDICTION DECLINED

§ 15. Assume we have determined that the court of our choice "has jurisdiction" in personam, in rem, or quasi-in-rem. Yet without further inquiry we cannot be certain that our court will "take" that jurisdiction in our case. The grounds on which it may refuse to do so are not easily classified. We may distinguish those situations in which the court *may* decline from those in which it *must* decline jurisdiction. However, it will be difficult to distinguish those cases in which a court "has" jurisdiction, but refuses to exercise it, from those in which it has no jurisdiction at the outset. The following sections will forego, therefore, any attempt at a logical classification. It will merely enumerate the most important situations in which a court, though free under the Constitution and the statutes of its state to take jurisdiction, will not do so in the exercise of a full or limited discretion.

1. FORUM NON CONVENIENS

§ 16–1. History. The doctrine of forum non conveniens is that a court having jurisdiction of a case will decline to exercise that jurisdiction, and thereby compel the plaintiff to sue elsewhere, if the forum is seriously inconvenient as a place to conduct the litigation. In the common law the doctrine is of relatively modern origin. Not until the last quarter of the nineteenth century was the need strongly felt for protecting the defendant against an overextended personal jurisdiction. This need was met by borrowing the doctrine of forum non conveniens from the law of admiralty. The doctrine has become law in most states and since 1947 in the federal courts. Gulf Oil (U.S. 1947). Rest.Conf.2d § 84; W 154–160; § 51. Wisconsin's long-arm legislation took the lead in giving the doctrine the stability of a statutory rule. And California, having incorporated such a statute in her provision establishing a jurisdiction going to the constitutional limit, may have shown the way to the development of a scheme of interstate venue in the forum conveniens (§ 4–16), to be implemented by trial and by error. See Buckeye (Cal.1969). State compacts may further promote dismissals on grounds of comity. Interstate Wrecking (N.J.1971).

§ 16–2. Admiralty. Perhaps owing to its long history, the practice of admiralty courts can be analyzed most readily. These courts have always exercised discretion in assuming or declining jurisdiction. However, the doctrine has exceptions that favor certain classes of plaintiffs. Dismissals are excluded in seamen's suits for wages under the Seaman's Act, and are extremely rare in suits by United States citizens. Jurisdiction will also generally be assumed in cases of termination of the voyage in the United States, unjust discharge without pay, undue deviation from the voyage agreed upon, lack of another forum for the plaintiff, or the master's cruel behavior. Hellenic Lines (U.S.1970). In addition plaintiff's presence in this country, lack of a foreign consul's readiness to grant relief, and nonapplicability of foreign law will ordinarily preclude dismissal. For a summary, see Grammenos (C.A.2, 1972). But the vitality of the principle, even concerning suits by American plaintiffs, is suggested by M/S Bremen (U.S.1972), infra § 23.

§ 16–3. General tests. The Supreme Court of California has stated: "In determining the applicability of the doctrine, the court must consider the public interest as well as the private interests of the litigants. The court must consider such factors as the ease of access of proof, the availability and cost of obtaining witnesses, the possibility of harassment of the defendant in litigating in an inconvenient forum, the enforceability of the judgment, the burden on the community in litigating matters not of local concern, and the desirability of litigating local matters in local courts. 'Unless the balance is strongly in favor of the defendant, the plaintiff's choice of forum should rarely be disturbed.'" Goodwine (Cal. 1965). On the relevance of choice of law, see Littmann (Wis.1973). Where "the plaintiff is a bona fide resident of the forum state . . . forum non conveniens has only an extremely limited application." Thomson (Cal.1967); W 154–158. See also New Amsterdam (Mass.1967). Where dismissal would force an American plaintiff into the court of a foreign country, forum non conveniens will usually not be applied. Olympic Corp (C.A.2, 1972 N.Y.); Rest.Conf.2d § 84. But see M/S Bremen (§ 17–2). The New York Court of Appeals has concluded that the "current rule—which prohibits the doctrine of forum non conveniens from being invoked if one of the parties is a New York resident—should be relaxed. Its application should turn on considerations of justice, fairness and convenience . . ." Silver (N.Y.1972).

New York courts ordinarily decline jurisdiction on foreign torts in suits *between nonresidents*. For other states, see e. g. Bekris (C.A.4, 1971

Va.); Yohanes (C.A.5, 1971 La.); Mid-Continent (Minn.1971).

§ 16–4. Conditional dismissal. A regrettable by-product of the application of the doctrine is delay, which may deprive the plaintiff of his remedy owing to the running of the statute of limitations. This risk can be avoided by a ruling that would *condition dismissal* upon the defendant's submission to the jurisdiction of the most convenient court, waiver of the statute of limitations, and possibly exact payment by the defendant of the plaintiff's counsel fees. See Interstate Wrecking (N.J.1971); AAE § 35. Upon such conditions dismissal may even be decreed in favor of extranational jurisdiction. Aetna Ins. Co. (N.Y.1967). Sanazzari (N.Y.App.1973). See also § 18–1. On the conditional stay of proceedings, see § 18–1.

§ 17. Federal transfer. For a brief period the federal courts had a decisional law rule of forum non conveniens. Gulf (U.S.1947). In 1948 the matter was regulated by statute, 28 U.S.C.A. § 1404(a). In federal courts a case may be transferred from one district to any other where it "might have been brought." 28 U.S.C.A. § 1404(a). Discretionary exercise of that power is not precluded by the prior dismissal of the same case by a state court on the ground of forum non conveniens. Res judicata is not applicable. Parsons (U.S.1963). Forum shopping by transfer has been reduced by the Court's ruling that a change of venue upon the defendant's motion under § 1404(a) generally should be "but a change of court rooms," and the transferee court is "obligated to apply the state law that would have been applied if there had been no change of venue." Van Dusen v. Barrack (U.S.1964). See Bott (C.A.5, 1971 Tex.). The Court reserved the question whether "the same considerations would govern if a *plaintiff* sought transfer under § 1404(a)." A negative answer in the defendant's favor seems likely. Carson (C.A.6, 1970 Ky.). The Court's second reservation concerned the case where "the transferor State would simply have dismissed the action on the ground of forum non conveniens." Van Dusen, supra.

The transfer provisions of 28 U.S.C.A. § 1404(a) apply only within the federal court system. The decisional rule of forum non conveniens can apply to dismiss an action in federal court that should have been brought in a court of some other nation. Fitzgerald (2d Cir. 1975).

2. FOREIGN ACTIONS

§ 18–1. Stay. A plaintiff may bring suits on the same cause of action in two or more different countries or states. In some cases the plaintiff's motive may be entirely legitimate, as where he desires to have his case tried under the most favorable law or most expedient practice, or where he finds property in another state on which he hopes to levy. But in general American courts are likely to stay proceedings pending the decision of prior suits on the same cause of action between the same parties, at least for a reasonable period. This practice has been commended by the Supreme Court. Kerotest (U.S.1951). Since the purpose is to protect the defendant from vexatious litigation, the primary test is whether on principles of res judicata and full faith and credit the foreign judgment will be recognized in the state of the forum for purpose of both enforcement and bar. This test is especially relevant for actions in rem and quasi in rem. Sanders (U.S. 1963). But the decision remains a matter of discretion for the trial court. Thomson (Cal.1967); Rest.Conf.2d § 86.

A stay may also be granted for the purpose of permitting the plaintiff to pursue his cause of action in a more convenient forum (§ 17–3), possibly with continuing jurisdiction in the first forum at least for a specified period, and upon compliance with certain conditions. Archibald (Cal. 1976).

Federal courts have authority to stay proceedings until the conclusion of actions pending in state courts on the same claim, even where such actions concern different parties. Mottolese (C. A.2, 1949 N.Y.).

§ 18–2. Abstention. A federal court in various circumstances may be permitted or required to abstain from exercising jurisdiction, in deference to the state courts. The doctrine of abstention can operate where the state court action is already pending, and plaintiff seeks a remedy concerning the same matter in federal court. Trainor (U.S.1977). The doctrine can also operate where the action is commenced in federal court but there is reason why it should have been brought in state court. R R Comm'n v. Pullman (U.S.1941). See § 51–5.

§ 18–3. Injunction. Another means to protect the defendant against a multiplicity of suits is an injunction against the plaintiff from proceeding elsewhere. Such injunctions will issue for example where the foreign suit was or is to be brought against a forum resident to evade a protection provided for him by forum law (e. g., exemptions or immunities), or to obtain a foreign divorce, or where a court has undertaken to administer an estate and a concurrent foreign action could affect the unitary administration. AAE § 36; W 159–160. Cf. Herman (N.Y.Sur.1972). But it will not suffice for a potential defendant to claim that he would receive a "less favorable consideration" in the other state. Brunzell (Nev.1965) (illegality of gambling in California). On the other hand, comity may induce a court to deny an injunction against a suit in the state of the situs. Humble Oil (C.A.4, 1968 S.C.).

A state court may not enjoin proceedings in a federal court; the remedy is to obtain a stay in the federal court. General Atomic (U.S.1978). Injunctions are not entitled to interstate recognition. Keck (Ill.App.1972); L § 55. "In certain situations", however, "comity" may be extended. Coyle (Pa.1970); also Monihan (Pa.1970). Yet, they may provoke counter-injunctions. James (Ill.1958). This practice is particularly frequent and invidious in matrimonial cases. Nowell (Tex.Civ.App.1966). In such cases foreign injunctions may be given effect "in the interests of equity, fair play and justice." Corbin (Conn.Super.1967). The law concerning injunctions against extranational divorces is summarized in Arpels (N.Y.1960).

4. INTERNAL AFFAIRS OF A FOREIGN CORPORATION

§ 19–1. General discretion. The assumption of jurisdiction over foreign corporations has been a gradual process. Having at first been treated as "nonexistent" (§§ 5, 27), they were later subjected to jurisdiction if "present" within the state. That jurisdiction has always excluded matters concerning their "internal affairs." But, except for such specific situations as actions to compel the declaration of dividends [Rogers (U.S.1933); Shuloff (C.A.2, 1963)], that exclusion has recently been subjected to discretionary principles akin to those governing the doctrine of forum non conveniens. Hoffman (C.A.3, 1970 Pa.); Lonergan (Ill.1967); Rest.Conf.2d § 84; Western Airlines (Cal.App.1961); § 84 Comment d; W 159.

§ 19–2. Specific rules. Some courts, on the other hand, have attempted to circumscribe the scope of their discretion. Thus, the New Jersey court has enumerated the following factors: "(a) whether the right sought to be enforced or protected is clear; (b) whether the judgment can be enforced; (c) whether enough parties are before the court to enable it to dispose of the entire controversy; (d) whether it would be more convenient for the parties to dispose of the case in the foreign jurisdiction; (e) whether the corporation has stockholders resident in states other than [the forum] and the state of the corporate domicile, thus giving rise to the possibility of disparate judicial determinations in a number of states; and (f) whether the controlling law of the corporate domicile state is doubtful or uncertain or the particular statute at the core of the controversy has not been definitely construed or its validity adjudicated in the home state." O'Brien (N.J. 1965).

5. LOCAL ACTIONS

§ 20. Under an ancient common law doctrine there is one type of action in personam that must be brought at the situs of a res, namely actions for trespass to land. Tracing this doctrine back to a 160 year old ruling [Livingston (C.C.Va. 1811)], the majority of states adhere to it as a mandatory rule of jurisdiction. Gibson (Ind. 1965). However, the rule is likely to lose this status in the future and to become just another facet of the doctrine of forum non conveniens. The rule has been criticized as inapposite to interstate relations and has been rejected by the courts of at least two states (Arkansas and Minnesota) and the legislatures of others (e. g., New York, Louisiana and Missouri). See Sarrica (N.Y.App. 1973). Moreoever, even where the rule survives it has often been limited to its narrowest confines. Rest.Conf.2d § 87; W 167; L § 49.

JURISDICTION EXCLUDED?

1. THE CONSTITUTION

§ 21. Full faith and credit. More than a half-century ago, the Supreme Court was called on to pass on a personal injury suit in Georgia of a railroad engineer against his employer. The suit was based on a statute of Alabama, the state of the accident. That statute provided that all actions under it "must be brought in a court of competent jurisdiction within the State of Alabama and not elsewhere." Defendant claimed that admission of the suit in Georgia would violate full faith and credit. The Court conceded that jurisdiction over a foreign statutory cause of action may indeed have to be denied "where right and remedy are so united that the right cannot be enforced except in the manner and before the tribunal designated by the act." Tennessee Coal (U.S.1914). But the Court avoided the result of this fateful dictum by finding that the claim involved a transitory cause of action. "A State cannot create a transitory cause of action and at the same time destroy the right to sue on that transitory cause of action in any court having jurisdiction . . . [under] the law of the court's creation." The circularity of this reasoning is obvious. For a cause of action can be found transitory only if it may be sued on elsewhere.

The Court's dictum has given rise to a host of problems. Thus, decades ago, the Supreme Court held that the common-law suit brought in New Hampshire by a Vermont employee against his Vermont employer for injuries suffered in New Hampshire, was subject to mandatory dismissal in full faith and credit to the Vermont workmen's compensation act which precluded the remedies sued for. Bradford Electric Light Co. v. Clapper (U.S.1932). Such dismissal presupposes, of course, that the law of the sister state is applicable to the cause of action.

However, the Supreme Court has said that it has "departed" from the Clapper rule. Carroll v. Lanza (U.S.1955); Rest.Conf.2d § 183. And, in a series of decisions adopting a flexible test of balancing state interests, the Court has upheld the forum's jurisdiction against the exclusionary statutes of (1) the place of injury [Alaska Packers (U.S.1935)]; (2) the place of contracting [Pacific Employers (U.S.1939)]; and (3) the place of the employer's domicile [Crider (U.S.1965)]. In Nevada v. Hall (U.S.1979), California was allowed to render judgment against Nevada, for an automobile accident caused by a state employee, despite a Nevada statute limiting such liability. That decision seems to put an end to any requirement that a state defer to another state's law where it has any Constitutional basis for applying its own law.

§ 22. Interstate and foreign commerce. Similarly, denial of jurisdiction with reference to the Interstate and Foreign Commerce clauses of the Constitution has gradually yielded to flexible standards approaching those of the doctrine of forum non conveniens (§ 17). In 1923 the Supreme Court found that a statute declaring the mere presence of a foreign corporation's agent sufficient to subject the corporation to jurisdiction on a foreign cause of action, imposed an unreasonable burden on interstate commerce. Davis (U.S.1923); W 151. But business activities of the defendant in the forum state have been consistently held to render suit by a resident plaintiff permissible. Dismissal will be limited to cases in which the litigation would impose an "oppressive and unreasonable" burden on the defendant. International Milling (U.S.1934).

The most recent decision on the problem indicates that the Commerce Clause may limit the reach of state court jurisdiction more narrowly than the Due Process Clause, but found no burden on commerce in the facts before it. Scanapico (2d Cir. 1970).

2. "OUSTER" BY AGREEMENT

§ 23. Prorogation. It used to be said that parties by their consent cannot "oust" any court of its jurisdiction. But this saying, even if it was ever true, does not state existing law.

Contractual ousters usually appear in agreements that also provide that any dispute arising under the contract shall be adjudicated in a specifically identified court. Such agreements may be called prorogation agreements in accord with international usage. After a long and tortured history, the Supreme Court now seems to have opened the door to a broad recognition of such agreements. In an action for the limitation of liability under American law, brought by an American tug owner against a German carrier and arising from a contract to tow a barge from Louisiana to Italy, the Court held prima facie valid a clause prorogating the High Court of Justice in London. M/S Bremen (U.S.1972). Future courts will have to determine the precise scope of this holding.

(1) Although the Court in part based its ruling on admiralty practice, it may have intended to cover "overseas commercial activities" in general. (2) Since the Court seemed primarily concerned with "the future development of international commercial dealings by Americans," it may have left unaffected *interstate* agreements. (3) The defendant will probably be permitted to show (a) that the agreement was not "freely negotiated" [see National Equipment (U.S.1964) 318, 333]; or (b) that foreign litigation would be "manifestly and gravely inconvenient [so that he would] be effectively deprived of a meaningful day in court." (4) "An agreement between two Americans to resolve their essentially local disputes in a remote alien forum" may or may not be denied effect. (5) The Court emphasizes that "the courts of England meet the standards of

neutrality and long experience in admiralty litigation." There remains the question, therefore, of whether less neutral, less experienced foreign courts will be equally favored. (6) Moreover, the Court expressly left open the possible impact of the forum's public policy. (7) Finally, availability of the prorogated court may or may not remain a condition for the agreement's effectiveness.

M/S Bremen follows a line of cases that recognize the validity of such agreements also between citizens. For the court in the leading case said that parties "might make any reasonable arrangement for the settlement of their disputes", and noted "the tendency in modern times . . . to permit greater freedom in contracting in matters of this kind than formerly." Mittenthal (Mass.1903) 426. This tendency should finally generally replace the old shibboleth against the "ouster" of courts from their jurisdiction. Accord, Scherk (U.S.1974); Reeves (Ore. 1972); Central Contracting (C.A.3, 1966 Pa.); W 163–165.

§ 24. Arbitration. Practically the most important instance of a court's contractual "ouster" from its jurisdiction is the old institution of the arbitration agreement. The history of these agreements is obscure. Although they have been usual among merchants ever since the 16th century, there have remained many traces of what is often regarded as a hostile attitude of judges jealous of their jurisdiction. Thus specific performance of the agreement is still far from being a matter of course. Rest.Conf.2d RS §§ 218, 219. But as with regard to ouster agreements in general (§ 23), the time has come for the abandonment of these relics of an outdated doctrine. Scherk (U.S.1974). Perhaps a statutory rule to this effect would be more readily acceptable if two possibilities of judicial control were clearly safeguarded: (1) to deny the validity of the agreement where unequal bargaining power or the use of forms cast doubt on the existence of true consent, and (2) to interpret the agreement as intended to lose its effect in the case of a change of circumstances. AAE § 43. See also Uniform Arbitration Act, 7 ULA 3 (1970, Supp. 1973) § 1, adopted in 15 states. Foreign arbitration treaties have been held not to exclude American jurisdiction. Joseph Muller (C.A.2, 1971 N. Y.).

An agreement to arbitrate under the United States Arbitration Act is specifically enforceable and is subject to specified judicial review. 9 U. S.C.A. §§ 4, 10, 11.

QUASI-JURISDICTIONAL DISMISSAL

§ 25. Suits are generally said to be subject to dismissal on "jurisdictional" or on non-jurisdictional (substantive or procedural) grounds. Only the former are usually included in discussions of jurisdiction. Yet the line is not easily drawn. Even the most clearly jurisdictional flaws (other than those concerning jurisdiction over the subject matter, § 4–1) may often be waived or otherwise cured. The essence of such flaws cannot, therefore, be found in their permanently impairing the validity of the judgment. On the other hand, "mere substantive" or "mere procedural" impediments of the cause of action or the parties, such as the running of the statute of limitations or lack of standing to sue or to be sued, are frequently said to "go to" the court's jurisdiction. The following pages will, therefore, discuss as quasi-jurisdictional some of the most important grounds for dismissal that are essentially independent of the merits of the case.

1. PROCEDURAL INCAPACITY

§ 26. The close affinity between jurisdictional and quasi-jurisdictional factors appears in the treatment of foreign corporations. Since it has been recognized that such corporations "exist" outside the state of their "creation" (§ 27–1), their standing to be sued has come to be phrased in terms of the court's jurisdiction. There are many related situations, however, with regard to both individuals and corporations which affect the parties' standing to sue (active capacity) and their standing to be sued (passive capacity) and which may or may not be discussed in jurisdictional terms.

A. Standing to Sue

§ 27–1. Corporations. At one time it was thought that "a corporation can have no legal existence out of the boundaries of the sovereignty by which it is created." Bank of Augusta v. Earle (U.S.1839). But corporations have long since been conceded standing to sue outside the state of their "creation." Certain exceptions persist. Some states still require reciprocity. Brown (Ga.1965). Also, a foreign corporation's standing to sue with regard to contracts concluded in the forum state may be conditioned upon its right to do business within that state. See Eli Lilly (U.S.1961). But see Allenberg Cotton Co. (U.S.1974) (foreign corporation doing interstate business is entitled to sue in state courts). And a shareholder's capacity to bring a derivative suit [see Eisenberg (C.A.2, 1971 N.Y.)] against a Venezuelan corporation was denied under Venezuelan law, the issue being treated as "substantive" under the conflicts law of New York, although procedural capacity is ordinarily governed by the law of the forum. Hausman (C.A.2, 1962 N.Y.).

§ 27–2. Unincorporated associations. Courts now, to an increasing extent, grant procedural capacity to such unincorporated associations as labor unions and cooperatives. But legislative support has sometimes been required, for example, in equating such associations with corporations for purposes of diversity jurisdiction (§ 50). United Steelworkers (U.S.1965); Rest.J.2d § 110.

§ 27–3. Dissolved corporations and associations. Courts will usually deny their capacity if either the law of dissolution or that of the forum permits such denial, unless a corporation qualifies under the former law as a "statutory successor." See § 28–4; AAE § 12. But courts of a "neutral state" may favor procedural capacity. Cheyenne (Del.1964).

§ 27–4. Individuals in general. Formerly, there were limitations on the capacity to sue of aliens, married women, infants, and prisoners. Limitations upon the *alien's* capacity have virtually disappeared, though many states require him to post security prior to being admitted to the court. *Civil death* by imprisonment, too, has been held a denial of equal protection. Payne (Cal.1976). *Minors, married women,* and *incompetent persons* have in general been treated under the law most favorable to them so that their active capacity is usually affirmed either under the law of the forum or under their personal law. The child's interest has been held paramount in granting a married woman standing to sue in a paternity suit against a man other than her husband. B. v. O. (N.J.1967). The problem is likely to disappear with the current progress in establishing full equality of women and children. Cf. Reed (U.S.1971). For the standing of foreign declarations of incompetency, see Sengstack (N.Y.1958); Delehanty (Ky.1969); Leathers (Ga. 1971).

§ 27-5. Representatives. There remains the reluctance to recognize the standing to sue of foreign-appointed *guardians* and *personal representatives.* It has been said that their procedural incapacity is "fundamental, going to the jurisdiction of the court." Hicks (Tex.Civ.App.1940). A few states have even maintained this incapacity by statute. Tolson (C.A.4, 1969 N.C.); Pantano (C.A.9, 1972 Ore.). This "nonrecognition" of foreign representatives, though a mere relic of history, has been justified by the forum's concern for local interests in local assets. But the rule has been riddled with so many exceptions that these exceptions are likely eventually to be accepted as the rule. Uniform Probate Code § 4-205(1969); L § 204. Thus failure to object to the foreign administrator's capacity has been held to result in a waiver of this objection. Summers (C.A.9, 1972 Ore.). See also Fed.R.Civ.Proc. 9(a). And the administrator has been given standing to sue as a holder in due course of negotiable instruments, as the trustee of the deceased's next-of-kin, and even as a matter of "comity."

§ 27–6. Receivers. Like the alleged incapacity of foreign personal representatives, that of foreign receivers seems ready for reexamination. There is an ever-growing number of exceptions promoted by practical considerations. AAE §§ 13–16.

§ 27–7. Indispensable parties. The starting point for determining which persons should be included as parties to a lawsuit is the common sense proposition that whenever feasible all persons materially interested in the case should be joined as parties. This permits all who are vitally concerned to be heard and helps to put the court in a position to do justice to all who have a stake in the controversy. When a person who should join as a plaintiff refuses to do so, he may be made a defendant or, in a proper case, an involuntary plaintiff. See e. g. Fed.R.Civ.Proc. 19(a).

But what if an interested person cannot be made a party because he cannot be served with process (e. g., he is neither a resident of nor a visitor within the state), or because, in a federal suit, his joinder would destroy the requisite diversity of citizenship (§ 50) or make the venue improper (§ 51)? Should the court go ahead without the joinder of such an interested person and do the best it can as among the joined parties? Or should it dismiss the lawsuit because of failure to include all materially interested persons?

Sometimes the presence in the lawsuit of the missing person has been considered so indispensable to its proper conduct that he has been designated an "indispensable party" and the case dismissed because of his absence. And sometimes the reason for such a dismissal has been couched in the terminology of "jurisdictional defect." Calcote (C.A.5, 1946). Prior to its reformulation in 1966, Fed.R.Civ.Proc. 19(a) provided that ". . . persons having a joint interest shall be made parties." Under this terminology the notion of indispensability was in part rooted in the absentee's assumed ownership of an inextricable "joint interest" in the subject matter of the lawsuit so that his rights inevitably would be affected by the judgment as though he were privy thereto in a res judicata or collateral estoppel sense (§ 29).

In 1966, Fed.R.Civ.Proc. 19(a) was rewritten to avoid the cryptic and conclusory labels of "joint interest" and "indispensable party" and focus instead on the practical legal consequences for parties joined and parties not joined. Revised Rule 19(a) provides that a person "subject to service of process and whose joinder will not deprive the court of jurisdiction over the subject matter of the action" shall be joined when necessary fully to dispose of the claims of the present parties and the person to be joined. Thus, a party shall be joined if "(1) in his absence complete relief cannot be accorded among those already parties, or (2) he claims an interest relating to the subject of the action and is so situated that the disposition of the action in his absence may (i) as a practical matter impair or impede his ability to protect that interest or (ii) leave any of the persons already parties subject to a substantial risk of incurring double, multiple, or otherwise inconsistent obligations by reason of his claimed interest." Nevertheless, the joined party shall be dismissed from the action if he "objects to venue and his joinder would render the venue of the action improper."

New Rule 19(b) grants the court discretion in deciding whether to proceed when a person who should be joined under 19(a) cannot be made a party. In making this decision, the court is instructed to consider the following factors: "first, to what extent a judgment rendered in the person's absence might be prejudicial to him or those already parties; second, the extent to which, by protective provisions in the judgment, by the shaping of relief, or other measures, the prejudice can be lessened or avoided; third, whether a judgment rendered in the person's absence will be adequate; fourth, whether the plaintiff will have an adequate remedy if the action is dismissed for nonjoinder."

This should make it clear that the question of indispensability is a practical one to be decided at the threshold of litigation, and not a "jurisdictional" defect that can overturn a judgment on appeal or later. Provident Tradesmens Bank (U.S.1968); Anderson (R.I.1971). However, some cases still hold that failure to join an indispensable party is a jurisdictional defect. Safeway Ins. Co. (Ill.App.1976).

B. Standing to Be Sued

(1) SOVEREIGNS

§ 28-1. United States. Certain persons have always enjoyed immunity from the courts' jurisdiction. Thus, the United States may not be sued without its consent, purportedly because there can be no right "against the authority that makes the law on which the right depends." Kawananakoa (U.S.1907). But there are many inroads into the rule. Thus, as early as 1797, "Congress decided that when the United States sues an individual, the individual can set off all debts properly due him from the sovereign. And

. . . Congress a hundred years ago created the Court of Claims, where the United States, like any other obligor, may affirmatively be held to its undertakings. This amenability to suit has become a commonplace in regard to the various agencies which carry out 'the enlarged scope of government in economic affairs' ". National City Bank (U.S.1955). For liberal interpretation of the congressional purpose in a suit for the return of seized enemy assets, see Honda (U.S.1967). See also Crown (U.S.1967) (statute of limitations in suit on government contract); § 45. For a discussion of *state* immunity, see Parden (U.S. 1964); Kenosha (Wis.1967); Nevada (U.S.1979); (sister state); concerning *Indians*, Security State Bank (Mont.1973).

§ 28–2. Foreign sovereigns. Such plaintiffs will be denied immunity with regard to their commercial operations and will be prevented from "invoking our law but resisting a claim against it which fairly would curtail its recovery." National City Bank, supra. With respect to commercial activity of foreign states, comprehensive legislation now removes the limitation of sovereign immunity subject to certain protective provisions. 28 U.S.C.A. § 1602 (Foreign Sovereign Immunities Act of 1976). The various types of *diplomatic* immunity are outside the scope of this book, since they pertain to public international law.

(2) CORPORATIONS

§ 28–3. Subsidiaries. Mere ownership by a foreign corporation in the stock of a subsidiary company resident in the forum state does not give the parent standing to be sued. Cannon (U.S. 1925). But hardship for the plaintiff is frequently alleviated by imputing the subsidiary's activities to the parent as constituting "doing business" in the forum state (§ 5). Boryk (C.A.2, 1965 N.Y.); Frummer (N.Y.1967); Farha (Kan.1975). But perhaps courts will begin to heed Judge Breitel's warning in the Frummer case, supra, that international difficulties might arise with regard to countries in which "the extension of jurisdiction projected in this case would hardly be tolerated." See Delagi (N.Y.1972); Conn (R.I.1969); Maryland Tuna (C.A.2, 1970); Rest.Conf.2d § 52.

§ 28–4. Dissolved corporations. We have noted the tendency to deny foreign dissolved corporations the standing to sue. The opposite tendency seems to prevail with regard to their standing to be sued, with and without reference to the appointment of a "statutory successor" in the state of incorporation. As to the latter, see Martyne (N.Y.1915); also Relfe (U.S.1880); Clark v. Williard (U.S.1934); Teague (Ark.1971). But this tendency favoring the standing to be sued seems to be limited to foreign dissolved corporations having assets or doing business within the forum state Bazan (Wis.1971). Rest.Conf.2d § 299.

§ 28-5. Unincorporated associations are in general treated like corporations. Rest.J.2d § 110.

(3) INDIVIDUALS

§ 28-6. Parties and witnesses. A *defendant* or witness will generally be held immune against service of process, while attending, or travelling to or from a court trial. See Lamb (U.S.1932); Crane (Fla.1971); W 161. But "the privilege is only extended as judicial necessities require". Eberlin (Pa.1961). See Fahy (Pa.Super.1972). Immunity protects even from arrest for contempt of court. Winter (Md.1967). Nor may any person be effectively served who was brought into the state by force. Croucher (Ill.App.1964); Rest.Conf.2d § 82. Similarly, jurisdiction will be defeated by any fraud the plaintiff may have committed directly or indirectly in obtaining service. See Commercial Mut. Acc. (U.S.1909); W 165; infra § 36-1(3). The Supreme Court would also protect *plaintiffs* present on court business because " 'courts of justice ought everywhere to be open'." Stewart (U.S.1916); Lyf-Alum (Wis.1966). But this immunity is not recognized in all states and, where recognized, is often limited. McCauley (Neb.1965). Nor is there agreement as to the immunity of *attorneys.* AAE § 31. Perhaps much could be gained by replacing rigid immunity rules through resort to dismissal under the doctrine of forum non conveniens (§ 17). See Wangler (N.J.1963); generally, Uniform Act to Secure the Attendance of Witnesses from Without a State in Criminal Proceedings, 9 ULA 87 (1931), adopted in nearly all states; W 162.

§ 28–7. Representatives. Among individuals it is again *guardians, receivers,* and *personal representatives* who offer the most important problems. With regard to their standing to be sued, even more clearly than with regard to their standing to sue (§ 27–5), the old rule assuming incapacity is on the wane. Thus, long-arm statutes (§ 4–5) have validly subjected to jurisdiction foreign personal representatives of persons who "submitted" to that jurisdiction by certain acts, typically the driving of a motor vehicle. NYCPLR § 302(a); Hayden (Ill.1965); also Gurley (C.A.5, 1972 Tex.); Barr (Kan.1969). Such statutes are constitutional. Peterson (Ga. 1966); Texair (Colo.1973); Tolson (C.A.4, 1969 N.C.); Rosenfeld (N.Y.1967). Uniform Probate Code, 8 ULA (1972) 571, §§ 4–301, 302, 303.

"Considerations of convenience and comity" and regard for "minimum jurisdictional contacts" [Jacobs (N.J.1957)] will be applied in exercising such statutory authority for the taking of jurisdiction.

Foreign *trustees* must be treated either like other individuals or as a "group" equivalent to an association. Danov (Minn.1963); AAE § 150. Civil law *"heirs"* are properly recognized as suable legal owners of the estate. Dubern (C.A.3, 1972 Pa.)

2. RES JUDICATA

§ 29. An earlier judgment may preclude a court from proceeding to the merits of a cause on several grounds and in several ways. Thus, a judgment in the plaintiff's favor has *merged* his cause of action and he cannot sue on it again in the same or any other court; any further action must be based on the judgment. If the judgment was against the plaintiff, it may *bar* him from another suit on the same cause of action. This is the rule of *claim preclusion.* Or, while having dealt with a different cause of action, the judgment in an earlier case may have decided certain questions of law or fact which cannot be re-tried. This is the rule of *issue preclusion* or *collateral estoppel.* In all these cases we speak of res judicata, thus using a term which is also frequently employed loosely to include such disparate institutions as the Law of the Case (precluding the appellate court from reconsidering its own rulings of law on a subsequent appeal in the same case) and Election of Remedies. The latter precludes a plaintiff who has chosen to pursue one of two mutually exclusive remedies from recovering upon the other. Rest.J.2d § 61.1, Comment m; Cook (Md.1971). The "Law of the Case" as declared in the same litigation "merely expresses the practice of courts generally to refuse to reopen what has been decided, not a limit to their power." Messinger (U.S.1912).

The effect of the first state's judgment is governed by the law of that state. See Aldrich (U.S.1963) (interstate); Schoenbrod (N.Y.1967); Watts (N.Y.1970) (international); infra § 36. Regarding judgments of two jurisdictions claiming recognition, see Treinies (U.S.1939); Rest. Conf.2d § 114; also Porter (C.A.9, 1969 Ariz.).

A. Merger and Bar

§ 30. Same cause of action. The most difficult problems raised by merger and bar are whether the causes of action and the parties are the same. The following tests help determine the "sameness" of the "causes of action": applicability of the same principles of substantive and procedural law; infringement in both actions of the same right by the same wrong; infringement of a right established in the first judgment by the judgment sought in the second action; identity of the evidence supporting both actions; and identity of the operative facts. Many of these tests are circular since they presuppose definition of the cause of action. Other tests are too vague. These include such broad and conflicting policy considerations as, on the one hand, preference for preclusion due to the desire to end litigation, prevent harassment by vexatious litigation, and generally secure reliance on established facts, and, on the other hand, acquiescence in relitigation compelled by the desire to give everyone his day in court. Decision from case to case is often the result of such conflicts. The Second Restatement substitutes the term "claim" for "cause of action" and declares the former "coterminous with the transaction" which in turn is to be determined by a "pragmatic standard." Rest.J.2d § 61, Comments a, b.

The problem is perhaps most dramatic where the two actions are brought in different states. Here workmen's compensation cases seem to have been litigated most frequently. The Supreme Court has apparently been increasingly concerned with the interest of workmen who, after having been improperly induced to bring their claim under an unfavorable statute, file another claim for the same injury in another state. The Court has moved away from its earlier holding against "double recovery" [Magnolia (U.S.1943)] to a more flexible formula by which the merger effect of sister state awards has been limited to the rare case of sister state laws expressly precluding additional relief. McCartin (U.S.1947). Other courts have sought to avoid the merger effect of the first award by assuming a new cause of action under their own law.

§ 31–1. Same parties. Merger and bar in and by an earlier judgment are limited to the parties and their privies. "Privity" for purposes of res judicata includes two basic kinds of relationship. First are substantive relationships—relationships among the parties in their out-of-court dealings that make it fair to treat one as representing the other in litigation with a third person. Rest.J.2d §§ 87, 89–110. Illustrations include owner and successor in interest in property, wherein a successor is bound by a judgment against his predecessor in title; stockholder and corporation, wherein the stockholders in a derivative suit are bound by a prior judgment against the corporation on the same cause of action; and bailee and bailor, wherein either is bound by a judgment against the other in an action against a third person to recover for the value of the bailed chattel.

The second kind of privity relationship is procedural—relationships wherein one party acts as representative of the other in litigation. Rest.J. 2d §§ 79–84. For example, if one party assumes control over litigation involving another, the controlling party is bound by issues determined in the litigation. So also a beneficiary of a trust is bound by litigation concerning the trust that is conducted by the trustee.

There is no clean line of distinction between these categories. The concept underlying both is that the identity of interest between the parties to the relationship is sufficiently close that a judgment against one may fairly be treated as binding the other.

§ 31–2. Class actions. The most tenuous form of privity is among the members of a class in a class suit. Yet, if the representatives adequately prosecute or defend, a class suit judgment is binding on the absent members of the defined class. Rest.J.2d §§ 85–86. "The procedure [must be] so devised and applied as to insure that those present are of the same class as those absent and that the litigation is so conducted as to insure the full and fair consideration of the common issue." Hansberry (U.S.1940); also Vasquez (Cal.1971). Fed.R.Civ.Proc. 23, as revised in 1966, codifies the historic rule that "the representative parties [must] fairly and adequately protect the interests of the class", and specifies in greater detail and with more precision the conditions of a class suit than did its predecessor. See now § 57.

§ 31-3. Administrators. There is one situation in which res judicata has been restricted by an artifical limitation of the privity concept. A foreign judgment against a foreign administrator may not be sued upon against a local administrator of the same decedent because of the alleged lack of privity between the decedent's representatives. The Supreme Court, apparently intent on protecting local interests, held in such a case that the local administrator was not barred. Ingersoll (U.S.1908). AAE § 64. But see Uniform Probate Code, 8 ULA 281 (1972) § 4-401.

B. Issue Preclusion

§ 32-1. Different cause of action. The rule of issue preclusion prevents a party from relitigating an issue he has previously and unsuccessfully litigated. The rule comes into play when a second action arises involving a different cause of action or claim but involving a common issue of fact or law. Thus, in a suit for a second installment of rent, it seems wasteful to permit the same parties to relitigate the validity of the underlying lease. Or in a suit for a second year's interest upon a note, it is hardly desirable to permit the reopening of questions concerning the original transaction, which were decided in a suit involving the first year's interest. According to the rule of issue preclusion a judgment on the merits "precludes relitigation of issues actually litigated and determined in the prior suit, regardless of whether it was based on the same cause of action as the second suit." Lawlor (U.S.1955); Rest.J.2d § 68. But preclusion is limited to "ultimate facts" and thus does not include facts which are only "evidentiary" in the second suit. Yates (U.S.1957). See also The Evergreens (C.A.2. 1944) ("mediate data"); Rest.J.2d § 68, Comment j.

Yet, even if the issue in the second suit was an ultimate fact necessary to the decision and identical with that in a prior suit, the court must take into account that "various considerations, other than the actual merits, may govern a party in bringing forward grounds of recovery or defence in one action, which may not exist in another action upon a different demand, such as the smallness of the amount or the value of the property in controversy, the difficulty of obtaining the necessary evidence, the expense of the litigation, and his own situation at the time." Cromwell (U.S.1877). Many attempts have been made, therefore, to adjust the scope of the "adjudicated issues" to the needs of individual justice, a problem which has proved particularly troublesome with regard to judgments by default and consent. Evershine (Ga.1972). In general, the courts have applied issued preclusion where, and only where, the causes of action, though not identical, were sufficiently related or similar so as to justify the conclusion that the party allegedly estopped could have been reasonably expected to litigate the issue in the first suit with the same vigor as in the second suit. See RS § 95 (law of the rendering court); Rest.J.2d § 68, Comment c.

A difficult question can be presented where the same issue arises successively in a state action and an action in federal court. In general, a federal court is required to give the same effect to a state court judgment as the state court would give it. 28 U.S.C. § 1738. However, federal policy may permit relitigation of an issue previously decided in state court. A state court determination on whether or not fraud existed in a contractual relationship is not preclusive when the issue subsequently arises in a federal bankruptcy proceeding. Brown (U.S.1979). A state court determination in a state race discrimination hearing may not be preclusive when the same issue arises in a subsequent federal adjudication. Cf. Alexander (U.S.1974). The underlying question is whether the scheme of federal remedies contemplates that the federal court may redetermine the issue notwithstanding the previous state court determination.

§ 32–2. Different parties-mutuality. Classically, a party who lost in the determination of an issue against one party could relitigate the issue in a subsequent action involving a third person. This followed from the doctrine of "mutuality." The "mutuality" rule was that a party who lost an issue was not bound against another person unless that other person would have been bound had the issue been decided the other way. Thus, if A sued B and won, and then C sued B on the same facts, B could relitigate the issue—because if A had lost C could still have relitigated the common issue. (The reason C could litigate the issue, of course, is that C was not a party to the first action and thus had never had his day in court.) The mutuality rule narrowly confined issue preclusion to the immediate parties to the first action, and those in privity with them. The effect was to allow a losing party to relitigate an issue that may have already been fully litigated against a prior adversary.

The mutuality rule was subject to a number of exceptions. Thus, a defendant whose liability is derived from or produces another person's (e. g. vicarious) liability, may, despite the absence of mutuality, successfully claim that other person's exoneration in the earlier judgment. Pinette (N.H.1965); Rest.J.2d § 99. Similarly, a plaintiff is estopped from suing the negligent employee after having recovered from defendant's employer on the same facts. Marange (Tex.Civ.App.1966); Massoth (Okla.1971).

The mutuality principle has now been abandoned altogether in most jurisdictions. The only condition for issue preclusion based on an earlier final judgment on identical issues is that "the party against whom the plea is asserted [be] a party or in privity with a party to the prior adjudication." Bernhard (Cal.1942), and that the early litigation have afforded a full and fair opportunity to litigate the issue. Rest.J.2d § 88. Thus a patentee is estopped to assert the validity of a patent that has been declared invalid in a prior suit against a different defendant, unless the patentee demonstrates that he did not have a full and fair opportunity, procedurally, substantively and evidentially, to litigate the validity of the patent in the prior suit. Blonder-Tongue (U.S.1971). Preclusion is applied both defensively—i. e., against a person who as plaintiff previously asserted the issue against another defendant—and offensively, i. e., against a defendant who lost the issue in a previous action by another plaintiff. Parklane Hosiery (U.S.1979). Rest.J.2d § 88.

But the "full-opportunity" rule, too, is not without exceptions. Thus, preclusion may be excluded where it would jeopardize the ascertainment of the truth without expediting the administration of justice. While a conviction for assault estops the defendant from relitigating the factual issue in a civil action for damages [Newman (Cal.App.1964)], an employer was permitted to relitigate the question of his employee's negligence which had been adjudicated in the latter's trial for manslaughter. The court found that "trial on the issues of contributory negligence and assumption of risk [not relevant in the criminal proceedings] required presentation of all of the evidence essential to a trial on the issue of negligence," so that a preclusion of the latter would be improper and fail to save expense. O'Connor (Cal.App.1967). So also, if the issue has been litigated with inconsistent results in two prior adjudications, it will not be treated as conclusively resolved. State Farm Fire (Ore.1976).

Conflicts questions may be troublesome. American courts will see grounds for "caution" when called on to find a party estopped by a judgment from a civil-law country with a fundamentally different approach to res judicata. See Bata (Del.1960); Carl Zeiss (C.A.2, 1970 N.Y.); AAE § 65.

On the other hand, within the federal system a court of one state is required to recognize the claim preclusive effects of a prior sister state judgment and, generally speaking, its issue preclusive effects as well. 28 U.S.C.A. § 1738; Treinies (U.S.1940).

3. STATUTE OF LIMITATIONS

§ 33–1. "Favor limitationis." The statute of limitations, once a disfavored defense, is now generally regarded as one of repose. Statutes of limitation assure that the administration of justice be not burdened and possibly misled by "stale" claims based on facts whose establishment has become difficult and unreliable. Little (N.C.1966). This policy has been implemented in several ways in interstate situations.

(1) The forum's shorter statute of limitations may be declared applicable as a matter of "procedure." Kershaw (Miss.1969); Mahalsky (C.A.6, 1972 Ohio); Michigan (Ariz.App.1972). See Rest.Conf.2d § 142(1).

(2) A foreign shorter period of limitations is frequently rendered applicable by "borrowing statutes," sometimes in terms of the Uniform Statute of Limitations on Foreign Claims Act. 9C ULA 161 (1967 Supp.) § 2.

(3) Even without borrowing statutes the foreign shorter period may be applied as "built-in" into the foreign cause of action. Davis (U.S. 1904); Gillies (C.A.5, 1972 Fla.); Gaston (C.A.5, 1968 Tex.); Alabama Great Southern (C.A.5, 1972 Miss.); Rest.Conf.2d § 143.

(4) So-called tolling statutes which suspend the running of the period of limitations, have of-

ten been held inapplicable to foreign claims or against nonresident defendants.

Application of a shorter forum statute against a sister state statute does not violate full faith and credit. Wells (U.S.1953). See NYCPLR § 202; Clarke (C.A.2, 1965 N.Y.). And equal protection is not denied by applying a shorter period against nonresidents. Horman (Cal.1971). Nor is such protection or full faith and credit denied by limiting suits upon sister state judgments to a period shorter than that applicable to domestic judgments. Watkins (U.S.1967); also McElmoyle (U.S.1839); Union Nat'l Bank (U.S. 1949); Rest.Conf.2d § 118.

§ 33–2. Favor actoris. Despite the general "favor limitationis," undue hardship for the plaintiff may be avoided in various ways. Thus, forum *residents* can be constitutionally favored. Canadian Northern (U.S.1920). And F.E.L.A. suits may be permitted in federal courts after the running of the federal statute if the suit had originally been commenced in a state court timely under the Act. Burnett (U.S.1965).

4. EXTINCTION ON DEATH

§ 34. Under the common law the death of either the injurer or the injured extinguished any action in tort, and no such action could be founded upon the injured's death. These rules have been modified in all states of the Union. "Revival" statutes entitle the court to take jurisdiction if an action by the decedent was pending at the time of his death, and "survival" statutes permit the bringing of a new suit upon the decedent's cause of action. Where the law of the forum differs from the law in which the cause of action accrued, courts now are inclined to prefer the law favorable to their jurisdiction. See Grant (Cal. 1953); AAE § 37. But if a court chooses to apply its non-survival rule as against a survival statute of the place of wrong, this has been held not to violate full faith and credit. Hartness (C. A.7, 1962 Ill.). For the question of active procedural capacity, see § 27–4.

5. PUBLIC POLICY

§ 35–1. In general. Unless the court is compelled by a constitutional mandate to take jurisdiction (§ 17), it is free to decline jurisdiction over a foreign cause of action on the ground that the claim brought before it violates public policy. NS § 18. For a long time the enforcement of foreign statutory tort actions was in itself considered opposed to the public policy of the forum unless the foreign law was sufficiently similar to that of the forum. This "provincialism" and similar rules have been abandoned. Loucks (N.Y. 1918).

§ 35-2. Direct actions. A typical example is the action under a statute which provides for direct action by an injured party against the injurer's liability insurer. Such an action may be constitutionally enforced by the enacting state even where the claim is based on an insurance contract which expressly outlaws such actions. Watson (U.S.1954). Another form of direct action is the suit through attachment jurisdiction against an insurer of the tortfeasor. See § 6-3. Such an action may be maintained in the plaintiff's state, assuming the insurer can be sued there, even if the tort occurred wholly in another state which would not permit such a suit. O'Connor (2d Cir. 1978).

§ 35-3. "Penal" actions. In addition to public policy the "penal" character of a foreign cause of action may be invoked to justify the court's refusal to enforce it. McGrath (R.I.1954); generally Huntington v. Attrill (U.S.1892). But this practice, too, is on the wane. It is particularly objectionable as causing undue hardship to the plaintiff where he is unable to obtain personal service in the state of the alleged accrual of the cause of action. Cf. Massachusetts Bonding (U. S.1956). On support claims, see § 38. Foreign "escheat laws are not penal and do not offend any policy" of the forum. Furman (N.J.1967); Rest.Conf.2d RS § 89.

JUDGMENT RECOGNITION (INTERSTATE AND INTERNATIONAL JURISDICTION)

1. MONEY JUDGMENTS

A. General Conditions

§ 36–1. Sometimes the defendant's entire property is located outside the territory of the court whose jurisdiction you intend to invoke. To proceed in that court will usually be advisable only if its judgment is entitled to recognition in the state or country of the situs. Such recognition among states will be based on Full Faith and Credit under the Constitution and among countries on international comity. Recognition depends on the fulfilment of several conditions.

(1) The judgment must be a *final* one. Compare Forslund (Vt.1963), with Ferster (Ga.1964). Finality is to be determined under the law of the rendering court. Maner (C.A.5, 1969 Ala.); Rest.Conf.2d § 107.

(2) The judgment must be *"on the merits."* Western Coal (Cal.1946); Rest.Conf.2d § 110; AAE § 63; supra § 30. A leading court has declared unenforceable, as violating the forum's public policy and indeed "fundamental principles of justice and fair play," a foreign judgment ob-

tained pro confesso under a cognovit or warrant of attorney. Atlas (N.Y.1969).

(3) The judgment must have been *fairly procured* and comply with certain minimum requirements of substantive propriety. AAE §§ 48–56; NS § 20. In particular fraud in the procurement of the judgment may be raised as bar to recognition to the extent of the relief provided by the rendering state. Baker (Kan.1967); Rodgers (Tex.App.1972); Rest.J.2d §§ 129–130. As to penal judgments (e. g. punitive damages), see e. g. Holbein (Fla.1971); 44 ALR 3d 960; as to tax judgments and assessments, NS § 18–2.

(4) Above all, the judgment must have been procured upon adequate notice, with valid territorial jurisdiction, and with jurisdiction of the subject matter of the action. Rest.J.2d § 4.

B. Interstate Jurisdiction

§ 36–2. The rendering court's jurisdictional finding. The rendering court's finding as to its jurisdiction will be treated as conclusive if complying with its own law and the United States Constitution. That is, its findings in this respect are conclusive under the rules of res judicata. This applies to findings concerning territorial jurisdiction and notice. Rest.J.2d § 13. Thus, if defendant makes a special appearance in State X, contending that the court lacks territorial jurisdiction, and the court finds that it does have such jurisdiction, defendant may not later relitigate that issue when the judgment is enforced in State Y. Gordon (Ga.1976). So also, if the defendant objects to the subject matter jurisdiction of the court, the court's determination as to its own jurisdiction is conclusive under almost all circumstances. Durfee (U.S.1963); Rest.J.2d § 15. The only qualification concerning subject matter jurisdiction is where the court's lack of jurisdiction is plain or allowing the judgment to stand would substantially infringe the authority of an agency of the federal government. Those conditions rarely arise. Kalb (U.S.1940).

However, when the judgment is by default, the rule of res judicata is inapplicable. Hence, in the recognition court the defendant may contest whether the rendering court had territorial or subject matter jurisdiction or gave adequate notice. Thompson (U.S.1874). Full opportunity to litigate the question of jurisdiction will be held sufficient even in international cases. Somportex (C.A.3, 1971 Pa.).

§ 36–3. Voluntary appearance. Anyone who "voluntarily appears, presents his case and is fully heard [is] thereafter concluded by the judgment of the tribunal to which he has submitted his cause." Baldwin (U.S.1931) (territorial jurisdiction). See also Chicot County (U.S.1940) (subject matter jurisdiction); Lacks (N.Y.1976) (divorce jurisdiction). This last principle (preclusion from attack by "participation") has been held applicable to divorce judgments even as to certain third parties. § 37–3; Rest.Conf.2d § 96.

§ 36–4. Scope of interstate jurisdiction. Even if the judgment court's jurisdictional finding has been held binding, another court may refuse the judgment recognition because of the type of jurisdiction found. Thus, an in personam judgment may be ineffective as to a res located elsewhere. The Supreme Court has held that a Nebraska court was not compelled to recognize a Washington decree ordering a husband to convey to his wife certain Nebraska land. Fall v. Eastin (U.S. 1909). But it may well be that this holding is limited to the facts of the case, i. e. to land decrees purporting to affect the title itself and to litigation involving third parties. Moreover, an in personam judgment concerning foreign land, though not entitled to full faith and credit, may even with regard to the adjudication of title still be given effect as a determination of the litigated issues, or at least of the facts and equities between the parties. Rozan (Cal.1957). And the forum's master in chancery may execute a conveyance ordered by a sister state court with personal jurisdiction over the defendant. Varone (C.A.7, 1966 Ill.). See also Zorick (Miss.1967) (collateral estoppel).

An in rem *default* judgment based on the assumed situs of the res within the rendering state, may be denied recognition in any other state which claims location of the res within its own territory. Thompson (U.S.1874). But if the issue of location of the res was litigated, that determination is conclusive. Durfee (U.S.1963).

§ 36–5. Federal courts. The Full Faith and Credit Clause technically is not operative among the federal district courts, for its provision is that "Full Faith and Credit shall be given in each State to the public Acts, Records and judicial Proceedings of every other *State*." U. S. Constitution, Art. IV, Sec. 1. But judgments of federal district courts are entitled to recognition by other federal courts and by state courts as a matter of federal law. Aerojet General (5th Cir. 1975). And in an action for the recovery of money or property, a judgment rendered in one federal district court may be registered in any other such court and upon registration has the same effect as though rendered in the court in which registered. 28 U.S.C.A. § 1963. However, a judgment so registered may not be enforceable insofar as it provides for an injunction. Stiller (C.A.2, 1963). And it is subject to the statute of limitations of the forum state. Matanuska (C.A.9, 1966 Wash.).

C. International Jurisdiction

§ 36-6. Domestic standards. With regard to extranational judgments, all courts reserve to themselves the right to apply their own standards of jurisdiction. In view of the absence of treaty obligations and in view of the ineffectiveness of uniform legislation, American courts are likely to refuse recognition to a foreign judgment which does not at least substantially conform to the requirements of due process. AAE § 59. For extreme cases applying such requirements to Canadian and Swiss proceedings and judgments, see Davidson (Nev.1973); Falcon (N.Y.City, 1967); Julen (Cal.App.1972).

§ 36-7. State law. State law rather than federal law is applicable to determine the scope of "comity." Somportex (C.A.3, 1971 Pa.). On this ground the reciprocity requirement as stated in a pre-Erie decision of the Supreme Court [Hilton (U.S.1895)], is no longer binding. Johnston (N.Y.1926). But cf. Kohn (E.D.Pa.1970). For collateral estoppel, see supra § 32; generally, Uniform Foreign Money-Judgments Recognition Act, 9B U.L.A. 66 (1966).

§ 36-8. International law. Regarding foreign expropriations, the Supreme Court has held that the "act-of-state doctrine" precluded judicial scrutiny in the absence of permissive executive action. Banco Nacional de Cuba v. Sabbatino (U.S.1964). Subsequently, however, Congress instructed the courts not to apply the doctrine in the absence of executive declarations to the contrary. AAE § 48(b). In 1972 the Court held the doctrine inapplicable where the executive branch of the government has stated that its application "would not advance the interests of American foreign policy." First National City Bank v. Banco Nacional de Cuba (U.S.1972).

2. DOMESTIC RELATIONS

A. Divorce

(1) SISTER STATE DECREES

§ 37–1. The domicile requirement in general. The rule now firmly established by the Supreme Court is that full faith and credit is only due to a decree of a domiciliary court. [Williams v. North Carolina (U.S.1945) (Williams II)], although "comity" recognition may be given in other cases.

Under this seemingly ironclad rule, interstate recognition could not be expected for decrees granted to non-domiciliaries whom the divorce court has held to have established a pseudo-domicile. The six-weeks quickie divorce of Nevada is the prototype of such *migratory* divorce decrees. "The burden of undermining the verity which the

Nevada decrees import rests heavily upon the assailant" [e. g. Ford (Vt.1971); March (Pa. 1967)]. However, the Supreme Court has maintained the principle that "the State of domiciliary origin should not be bound by an unfounded, even if not collusive, recital [of domicile] in the record of a court of another State". Williams II; § 9-2. A migratory decree, however well-founded in the divorce court's (local) jurisdiction, therefore may be successfully attacked in any other state and, upon remarriage, may not even be effective protection against prosecution for bigamy. On the other hand, the Rhode Island court upheld a Nevada divorce despite a subsequent Massachusetts judgment declaring it "invalid and void." Rymanowski (R.I.1969).

§ 37-2. The Uniform Act. Attacks against the divorce court's domiciliary findings have been encouraged by the Uniform Divorce Recognition Act [9 U.L.A. 461 (1965)] which, in ten jurisdictions, has been in effect for at least twenty years. "Proof that a person obtaining a divorce . . . in another jurisdiction was (a) domiciled in [the forum state] within twelve months prior to the commencement of the proceeding therefor, and resumed residence [in that state] within eighteen months after the date of his departure therefrom, or (b) at all times after his departure from [the forum state] and until his return maintained a place of residence" therein, was declared "prima facie evidence that the person was domiciled [in the forum state] when the divorce proceeding was commenced" (§ 2). And "a divorce . . . obtained in another jurisdiction shall be of no force or effect [in the forum state], if both parties . . . were domiciled [in the forum state] at the time the proceeding for divorce was commenced" (§ 1). But, with minor exceptions [e. g. Yost (Nev.1955)], the Act does not seem yet to have been applied to invalidate a sister state divorce decree.

§ 37–3. Consent (bilateral) divorces. Apparently concerned with post-divorce marriages that are exposed to attack, the Supreme Court has created a subterfuge for such marriages which in effect has largely superseded the Williams rule and produced a new institution of divorces by consent. The Court has held that "the requirements of full faith and credit bar a defendant from collaterally attacking a divorce decree on jurisdictional grounds in the courts of a sister State where there has been participation by the defendant in the divorce proceedings, where the defendant has been accorded full opportunity to contest the jurisdictional issues, and where the decree is not susceptible to such collateral attack in the courts of the State which rendered the decree." Sherrer (U.S.1948). This preclusion of collateral attack has been extended to operate against *third parties* who have not themselves participated in the "consent" divorce, if the law of the rendering court so provides. Johnson v. Muelberger (U.S.1951). See Schoenbrod (N.Y. 1967). Whether prosecution for bigamy is equally precluded by such divorces remains an open question. AAE § 74.

Another open question concerns the impact of the *Uniform Divorce Recognition Act* (§ 37–2) on "consent divorces." The "no-force-or-effect" clause has been held not to invalidate such divorces. Dietrich (Cal.1953). Indeed, even beyond the reach of full faith and credit, state *estoppel* rules have been given wide application, Rest.Conf.2d § 74, while *federal* legislation may require more stringent enforcement of the domicile requirement. Mott (C.A.3, 1969) (social security). And *foreign* countries usually refuse recognition to all migratory divorces. PIL § 267–1.

(2) EXTRANATIONAL DIVORCES

§ 37–4. Ex parte (unilateral) divorces. Some states have reserved complete discretion to grant or deny recognition to any extranational divorce, without feeling committed to "comity." Kittel (Fla.App.1967). In any event, mail order divorces will certainly remain wholly void as lacking "even the slightest color of jurisdiction." Caldwell (N.Y.1948). Cf. Unruh (Ariz.1956) ("quasi estoppel").

Even the spouse who has procured the unilateral divorce may attack it. Zeitlan (N.Y.App. 1967). Cf. Diehl (C.A.5, 1971 Tex.). And extrinsic fraud may be claimed as it may against any other judgment. Tamimi (N.Y.App.1972). Regarding injunctions against the procurement of unilateral divorces, see § 18–2; PIL § 269; and regarding the preclusion of attack by laches, see Krieger (N.Y.1969).

§ 37–5. Consent (bilateral) divorces. In the United States a decision of the New York Court of Appeals may represent a turning point. The husband had obtained a divorce decree in Mexico in compliance with the local "residence" requirements and his wife had voluntarily appeared. The court upheld the divorce because "a balanced public policy now requires that recognition of the bilateral Mexican divorce be given rather than withheld and such recognition as a matter of comity offends no public policy of this state." Rosenstiel (N.Y.1965). Several states have followed suit. McCarthy (Mass.1972); Perrin (C.A.3, 1969 Vir.Isl.); W 190–191. The Uniform Act (§ 37–2) has not so far affected that practice and is unlikely to do so. Kakarapis (N.Y.Fam. Ct.1968). And the Hague Convention of 1968 on the Recognition of Divorces and Legal Separations, though not adhered to by the United States, has accommodated extranational divorces of Americans in several ways. PIL § 267–3.

(3) EFFECT ON POST–DIVORCE SUPPORT

§ 37–6. Whatever be the effect of a migratory ex parte divorce decree on the marital status, it seems clear that such divorces cannot affect the out-of-state spouse's right to support. This is so whether such right be one previously established by judicial decision, or one whose adjudication is sought subsequent to the divorce, provided always that the law of the state in which the right to support is in issue, recognizes such a right. Estin (U.S.1948); Vanderbilt (U.S.1957); Morphet (Ore.1972). Ordinarily, the latter law is that of the dependent spouse's domicile. Worthley (Cal. 1955). The Uniform Act (§ 38–2), however, has been held to render determinative the lex fori as such. Rymanowski (R.I.1969).

The Estin rule even permits a migratory spouse to claim alimony after an ex parte divorce. Mandelberg (Nev.1972). AAE §§ 79–81. However, in Simons (U.S.1965), it was held that an ex parte divorce could extinguish a right of dower. And a migratory divorce based on personal jurisdiction will extinguish the right to post-divorce support existing under the law of the forum and domicile if the law of the divorce court so provides. Kresteff (Ill.App.1967). This rule will even be applied to Mexican divorces. Lappert (N.Y.1967) (dictum). Concerning the enforcement of foreign decrees, see infra § 38.

B. Support

§ 38–1. In general. At one time support problems were considered as of local concern only and "of no special interest to other states." Rest. Conf. § 458, Comment (a). This time is past. It has long been clear that a support judgment as to accrued installments which is not subject to modification by the rendering court, is entitled to full faith and credit in other states. Sistare (U.S. 1910); Lumpkins (N.M.1972). Moreover, even a modifiable judgment may be entitled to recognition, provided such recognition would not affect the defenses which would have been available to the defendant in the rendering court. Griffin (U.S.1946); Schoch (Cal.App.1970). On the other hand, decrees for future support which are quite generally subject to modification, are not entitled to recognition. Hendrix (Conn.1970). But cf. McGuire (Ga.1972). But even such decrees can in some states be "established" as domestic decrees. Worthley (Cal.1955); W 187–188. And reservation, by a sister state court, of jurisdiction to carry out a support agreement does not deprive the forum of jurisdiction to order compliance with the sister state judgment based on that agreement. Lipman (Mass.1965).

§ 38–2. Uniform Act. The Uniform Reciprocal Enforcement of Support Act has been amended three times, lastly in the Revised Uniform Reciprocal Enforcement of Support Act 1968. E. g. Craft (N.D.1970). Each version having been adopted and retained in overlapping groups of states and the Act has raised "many confusing questions [which] have not yet been resolved." Davidson (Wash.1965); AAE § 143; NS § 38. This confusion may account for the provision that a decree obtained under the Act will not supersede a previous one. Howard (Miss.1966). Concerning the registration procedure, see supra § 9–2; AAE § 84; and, in general, Brockelbank and Infausto, supra § 9–2.

C. Children's Custody

§ 39. Lack of finality, we have seen (§ 38–1), has deprived support orders of their enforceability in other states. In strange contrast, custody decrees, which everywhere may be modified to further the child's welfare and thus always lack finality, are widely attributed such enforceability under the Full Faith and Credit Clause. MacMillan (Colo.1971); Faris (Ill.1966); Bussey (Nev.1972); Bahr (S.D.1970); Knowles (Tex. 1969); Rankin (Wash.1969). This may in part be due to the courts' desire to restrain parents who have been denied custody in one state, from seeking a more favorable adjudication in another state in disobedience of the first order. Yet, courts of all states have always had to adjust this seemingly rigid principle to the changing needs of the child's welfare. They have done so by either denying the first court's "jurisdiction" or by finding a change of circumstances since the issuance of that court's decree. But other courts have already found that "the full faith and credit clause does not apply to custody decrees." Bachman (N.Y.1956). See also Hicks (Kan.1972); Batchelor (Ky.1966); Hawkins (Ore.1972); W 196–197. Rightly or wrongly, the petitioning parent's "clean hands" will play a role in the courts' redetermination of a custody issue. Ferreira (Cal. 1973); W 197–199.

D. Adoption

§ 40. While the condition and effects of marriage and filiation are substantially identical throughout the Western world, relationships based on adoption may have little in common but the name. Also, adoption proceedings vary from judicial decree, through mere contract, to "virtual" adoption, adoption by "estoppel," and "equitable" adoption. Handley (Ga.1968). These facts have greatly hampered the development of a uniform practice concerning both the assumption of domestic jurisdiction (§ 12) and the recognition of adoptions outside the state of their "creation." PIL §§ 312–324.

In general the problem has been raised in terms of the adoption state's jurisdiction to "create" the adoptive status (§ 12). Such "status" language will generally suffice to attach forum incidents to foreign transactions in the adoptee's favor. Rest.Conf.2d § 290; PIL § 310. See Akin (C.A.5, 1963 La.); Delaney (N.M.1963); Stellmah (N.J.1966). But cf. O'Dea (Cal.App.1973). Even a jurisdictionally valid foreign adoption may in certain respects be denied effect. Montgomery (C.A.8, 1962) (immigrant's admissibility). See Hood (U.S.1915); NS § 114. The adoption court's alleged jurisdiction in rem may be impeached if it was acquired without notice to the natural parents [O'Dea (Cal.App.1973)], though such jurisdiction may be upheld in the case of proved abandonment. AAE § 51.

CRIMINAL JURISDICTION

1. TERRITORIAL JURISDICTION

§ 41. "The common law considers crimes as altogether local, and cognizable and punishable exclusively in the country, where they were committed." Story, Conflict of Laws 516 (1834). This so-called territorial principle rests on the ancient guarantee that every defendant must be tried by a jury of the county or vicinage in which the crime was committed. Story's rule may be taken as the starting point for analysis of the law prevailing in this country today, but the more general application of this principle in interstate and international relations is not easily justified and far from generally accepted internationally. An ever increasing number of exceptions expanding criminal jurisdiction require caution.

In the first place, arrest for felonious acts may take place in states other than that of the crime. Klein (Wis.1964). Moreover, a citizen of the United States, by virtue of the obligations of such citizenship, may, if a statute so prescribes, constitutionally be prosecuted in this country for any crime against it committed abroad. See Blackmer (U.S.1932); Skiriotes (U.S.1941). Conversely, a foreign court's jurisdiction over its own citizens will be recognized though the alleged crime was committed in this country, even if the defendant was also a citizen of the United States. Coumas (Cal.1948).

Prosecution for treasonable acts committed abroad is founded on U.S.Const. Art. III, § 3, and with regard to aliens "owing allegiance to the United States" on 18 U.S.C.A. § 2381. Carlisle (U.S.1873). So far, jurisdiction over aliens committing hostile acts against the United States in a foreign country has not been claimed. See Kawakita (U.S.1952) (a dual national). Recently the civil jurisdiction of American courts over acts committed abroad in violation of American antitrust laws has been much discussed. It is now understood that the question is merely "whether

Congress chose to attach liability to the conduct outside the United States of persons not in allegiance to it." Aluminum (C.A.2, 1945). For a similar development in the area of Securities Exchange regulation, see e. g. Travis (C.A.8, 1973). The tendency in these fields extensively to interpret Congressional powers and aspirations may yet lead to a broadened conception of criminal jurisdiction over the acts of nonresident aliens abroad. Federal criminal jurisdiction will be dealt with in § 46.

Other modifications of the territorial principle are the result of the difficulty of localizing international and interstate crimes. In a case involving a multi-state conspiracy, the Supreme Court summarized the rule of Armour Packing (U.S. 1908) to the effect that "the Sixth Amendment . . . providing that an accused shall be tried in the state and district where the crime is committed, [does] not preclude a trial of the offense [transportation of merchandise for less than the published rate] in any of the districts through which the transportation was conducted." Hyde (U.S.1912). And a state may punish acts preparatory to the commission of a crime outside the state. See e. g. Burt (Cal.1955); Anderson (Cal.1961). Tickle (N.C.1953) (place of the child's birth); also § 42. Jurisdiction in such situations, of course, always depends on the interpretation of the penal statute of the forum.

2. "PERSONAL" JURISDICTION

§ 42. In general, criminal jurisdiction is predicated on the defendant's presence in the state. That jurisdiction is not impaired by the fact that this presence was unlawfully obtained. Mahon (U.S.1888). Presence must continue throughout the proceedings, but the right of physical presence in the courtroom of course presents additional considerations; such right in effect may be waived by a defendant's disruptive conduct. Allen (U.S.1970). Where the offender has fled the country, his presence may be secured by extradition treaty. In interstate relations the delivery of those who "flee from justice" is provided by the Constitution. U.S.Const. Art. 4, § 2. The federal duty imposed on the governor of the state from which extradition is demanded is a moral obligation only. No judicial power in the federal government compels him to perform it. Kentucky (U.S.1861).

The Uniform Criminal Extradition Act, adopted in most states, and the Interstate Agreement on Detainers in which at least forty states have joined, purport to go further than the federal constitution. Section 6 of the Act provides for extradition where an act resulted "in a crime in the [demanding] state, . . . even though the accused was not in that state at the time of the commission of the crime," and therefore has not, by his continued absence, "fled from justice." The enforcement of this provision may be hampered, however, by decisions which perhaps have given constitutional effect to the principle of territoriality. Thus, as late as 1963, the New Hampshire court, apparently on this theory, refused extradition of a forum citizen to Massachusetts which claimed jurisdiction in a criminal support and paternity case concerning a child within its territory. Chief Justice Kenison, dissenting, objected forcefully to this decision as an outgrowth of "rigid dogma" which would make an important legislative remedy inapplicable "in support cases where it is most needed." Hardy (N.H.1963). Perhaps the court's decision in Hardy really is rooted in the notion that the states may not in their extradition laws exceed the scope of the federal constitutional provision. But in Brito (Neb.1964) it was held that "Since Congress may legislate only on subjects authorized by the Constitution, and since powers not expressly delegated to the United States by the Constitution are reserved to the states, it should follow that if a person has not fled from the demanding state, this field is left to the states. In any event, Congress has not attempted to legislate in this area, and at least 44 of our states have done so by the adoption of section 6 of the Uniform Criminal Extradition Act." See Wertheimer (Minn. 1972); AAE § 82.

A special kind of jurisdiction, namely that over *military personnel*, is beyond the compass of this book. Important limitations on this jurisdiction have been articulated by the Supreme Court of the United States. It has been held, for example, that the Uniform Code of Military Justice extending court-martial jurisdiction to persons accompanying the armed forces abroad could not be constitutionally applied to the trial of civilian dependents of members of such forces in times of peace. Reid (U.S.1957); also Kinsella (U.S. 1960); McElroy (U.S.1960).

VENUE

§ 43. An essential element in the theory and practice of litigation concerns the venue of the lawsuit, that is, the proper place for its commencement and trial. In American state practice the problem typically is as to the proper county, but there may be additional problems as to the proper district or branch within the proper county. The venue problem in federal court is treated in § 51.

The basic venue rule in virtually all states is that a defendant normally should be entitled to have a case against him tried in the county of his residence if the case involves a transitory as distinguished from a local cause of action. J. & H. § 12.3. The rationale is that a person legally attacked is entitled to fight on his home territory. But there are many countervailing or at least intercepting rules whereby *the* proper or *a* proper venue—for often more than one venue is a proper one—may be the county where the tort was committed, or the contract entered into, or where the estate is located or administered which a defendant executor, administrator, guardian or trustee represents. J. & H. § 12.3. Generally, the court has power within its sound discretion to remove a case from one proper county to another county more appropriate for the convenience of witnesses and the ends of justice. 74 A.L.R.2d 16.

The absence of proper venue ordinarily does not go to the court's jurisdiction. For such absence does not prevent a valid judgment unless appropriate objection is seasonably made. But there are important exceptions to this waiver principle, exceptions which are the reason for the inclusion of venue in this text. For example, until recently the California Constitution, former Art. VI, § 5, provided a clear illustration of constitutional, non-waivable venue. That section until 1966 required that all actions for the recovery of the possession of real estate, or quieting title thereto, or enforcement of liens thereupon be commenced in the county in which the affected real estate, or any part of it, is situated. This was truly a jurisdictional limitation, for an action of the kind specified could not go to a valid judgment except in a proper county. Rogers (Cal. 1894). Under such a rule a cause of action could well have been barred by the statute of limitations by the time a complaint was filed in the proper county, even though the initial complaint in another county had been timely filed. Fortunately in the constitutional revision of 1966 Art. VI, § 5 was deleted, so that now local actions are wholly statutory in California. Cal.C.Civ.Proc. § 392(1).

Other venues, too, sometimes are regarded as jurisdictional, e. g. the venue in probate proceedings in that county in which the decedent resided or had property at the time of death; or the restriction on issuance of writs of habeas corpus to the court of the county of petitioner's custody. Rest.J.2d § 7, Comment h. The venue of state courts may also be prescribed by mandatory federal statutes. Mercantile Nat'l Bank (U.S.1963) (national banks). On venue agreements, see § 23.

FEDERAL JURISDICTION

§ 44–1. Introduction. Federal Jurisdiction is a specialty and a law school subject of its own—an interesting, intricate and challenging one. For a fuller concise treatment, see Currie, Federal Jurisdiction in a Nutshell (1976).

§ 44–2. "Cases and controversies." At the threshold must be noted the limitation of federal jurisdiction to actual *"cases"* and *"controversies."* U. S. Constitution, Art. III, Sec. 2. The restriction of the jurisdiction of the United States District Courts to actual "cases" and "controversies" is basic constitutional doctrine, inherent in the concept of separation of powers. Marbury (U.S. 1803). Thus advisory opinions are precluded. Muskrat (U.S.1911); cf. McGrath (U.S.1950). Although it was once doubted that declaratory judgment actions present justiciable controversies [Willing (U.S.1928)], such actions are now expressly authorized by Congress in "a case of actual controversy" [28 U.S.C. § 2201; Fed.R. Civ.Proc. 57], and the authorization is clearly constitutional. Aetna Life Ins. Co. v. Haworth (U.S.1937).

§ 44–3. Standing to sue. Generally there is no justiciable controversy if plaintiff's status to complain is only that of a federal taxpayer [Frothingham (U.S.1923)], although the rule may be different if plaintiff complains as a municipal or state taxpayer [Everson (U.S.1947); Wieman (U.S.1952)]. Even a federal taxpayer may have standing if he is attacking a federal spending program under a constitutional provision which operates as a specific limitation upon the exercise by Congress of the taxing and spending power. Flast (U.S.1968). To have standing a complainant must show actual injury, whether of an economic [Data Processing (U.S.1970)] or environmental [Sierra Club (U.S.1972)] nature. If a dispute is otherwise justiciable, Congress may determine who is a "proper party to request an adjudication of a particular issue." Flast, supra. When the plaintiff's injury is remote, standing may depend on whether Congress confers standing on persons in plaintiff's situation. Warth (U.S.1975). Realistically, standing often depends on whether the merits of plaintiff's case are regarded with favor. Simon (U.S.1976).

§ 44-4. Political questions. Mere political questions, such as whether a state has the constitutionally required republican government, do not present justiciable controversies. Luther (U.S. 1849). But whether apportionment of a state legislature denies equal protection of the law has been held to present such a controversy. Baker (U.S.1962); Reynolds (U.S.1964); Kilgarlin (U. S.1967); cf. Gray (U.S.1963) (county-unit system for election of state officials condemned); Fortson (U.S.1966) (election of governor by general assembly when popular election fails, upheld); Sailors (U.S.1967) (method of selection of boards of education was basically appointive and "one man-one vote" principle irrelevant). Holshouser (M.D.N.C.1971); Wells (U.S.1973) (election of state judges and one man-one vote principle). Challenges to apportionment of congressional districts are now justiciable. Wesberry (U.S.1964).

§ 44–5. Borderlines. The doctrines and distinctions developed in implementation of the restriction of jurisdiction to justiciable controversies, produce inconsistent holdings. For example, compare Doremus (U.S.1952) (no justiciable controversy presented by local taxpayers' attack on public school reading of parts of the Old Testament), with Engel (U.S.1962) (justiciable controversy presented by local taxpayers' attack on New York Regents' prayer). See Wright, Federal Courts 42 (2d ed. 1970).

The refinements, complications and inconsistencies of the "actual" controversy doctrine and its corollaries typically are pursued in detail in courses in Constitutional and Administrative Law. In the latter area the problem of justiciability often is essentially one of the timeliness of judicial intervention in the processes of administrative agencies—whether the complainant has first exhausted his administrative remedies [Myers (U.S.1938)], or whether the controversy is ripe for review [Columbia System (U.S.1942) (dissent)]. The problem also may be one of primary jurisdiction, that is, whether an administrative agency or a court should make the initial determination. Texas & Pac. Ry. (U.S.1907); cf. California v. Federal Power Commission (U.S. 1962).

Before turning to the kinds of jurisdictional problems that this text is chiefly concerned with —those arising in the every day controversies between individuals, corporations and other private entities, nowadays generally called "civil suits"— we note four distinct and important occupations of our federal courts: (a) government litigation, i. e. civil suits to which the United States government is a party; (b) bankruptcy proceedings; (c) criminal cases; and (d) admiralty suits.

1. SPECIAL JURISDICTIONS

A. Government Litigation

§ 45–1. United States as plaintiff. U. S. Constitution, Art. III, Sec. 2, provides that "The judicial power shall extend . . . to controversies to which the United States shall be a party." This constitutional authorization is implemented by 28 U.S.C.A. § 1345, according to which, except as otherwise provided by Act of Congress, the United States District Courts "shall have original jurisdiction of all civil actions, suits or proceedings commenced by the United States, or by any agency or officer thereof expressly authorized to sue by Act of Congress." Congress by various statutes has authorized the United States or its agencies or officers to sue. But even without specific authorization the Government may have standing to sue, as where a suit is necessary to protect the general welfare. Debs (U.S.1895).

Sometimes the federal jurisdiction is exclusive, e. g. 28 U.S.C.A. § 1355 (actions for fines, penalties or forfeitures under Act of Congress). But much of the federal court jurisdiction of actions begun by the United States is concurrent with that of the state courts.

§ 45–2. United States as defendant. While the jurisdictional basis for suits when the United States is plaintiff is thus clear, the problem is much more complicated when the United States is named as a defendant. For the controlling principle then is the notion that a sovereign cannot be sued without its consent. See also § 28. For years now the notion of sovereign immunity has been eroding away. The United States has now consented to numerous kinds of suits against it, e. g. suits to recover taxes, 28 U.S.C.A. § 1346(a), and for certain torts, 28 U.S.C.A. § 1346(b).

B. Bankruptcy Proceedings

§ 45–3. 28 U.S.C.A. § 1334 provides that the United States District Courts shall have original jurisdiction, exclusive of the courts of the States, of all matters and proceedings in bankruptcy. The Congressional power so to provide is not based on the Judiciary Article of the U. S. Constitution, Art. III, but rather on Art. I, Sec. 8, which provides, inter alia, that "The Congress shall have power . . . to establish . . . uniform laws on the subject of bankruptcies throughout the United States." National Mutual Ins. (U.S.1949). Whenever a federal bankruptcy act has been in effect—the first was enacted in 1800, and we have had one continuously since 1896—the United States District Courts as bankruptcy courts have had exclusive jurisdiction over bankruptcy proceedings.

C. Criminal Cases

§ 46-1. The Constitution. The United States as a sovereign has jurisdiction or power to punish offenses against it. For a discussion of the general principles of territorial limitation on criminal jurisdiction, and exceptions thereto in the case of the United States, see § 41. The United States Criminal Code, 18 U.S.C.A., is replete with criminal statutes, ranging all the way from one on treason, U. S. Constitution, Art. III, Sec. 3, to one proscribing the mailing of obscene matter, 18 U.S.C.A. § 1461. A modernization of the Criminal Code is now in progress. In addition to the criminal statutes which, growing out of the federal government's status and functions as such, Congress has used among other powers the Interstate Commerce Clause to bring within federal jurisdiction criminal conduct which otherwise would be in the exclusive domain of the states. For example, the taking across state lines of kidnapped persons, 18 U.S.C.A. § 1201, of stolen property, 18 U.S.C.A. §§ 2311-18, and of women for immoral purposes, 18 U.S.C.A. § 2421, are federal crimes. Cf. Tot (U.S.1943). More recently Congress has prohibited under criminal sanctions interstate travel for purposes of inciting riots. 18 U.S.C.A. § 2101. Other penal sanctions, e. g. to control the drug traffic, have long been justified under the federal taxing power. Doremus (U.S.1919). By reason of 18 U.S.C.A. § 3231, the United States District Courts have original jurisdiction, exclusive of the courts of the states, of all offenses against the United States.

It is commonly assumed that the constitutional basis for this is Art. III, Sec. 2's extension of the federal judicial power to "all Cases . . . arising under . . . the laws of the United States." Since there are no common law crimes against the United States and a federal prosecution must therefore be based on a federal statute [United States v. George (U.S.1913)], this is an adequate constitutional basis both for prosecutions commenced in the federal district courts and probably also for the relatively few prosecutions removable from state to federal court, e. g., where a federal official is prosecuted by a state for an alleged crime committed under color of the federal office or under authority of federal law. 28 U.S.C.A. § 1442; Tennessee v. Davis (U.S. 1880). Another constitutional basis perhaps adequate to support jurisdiction of original federal prosecutions is Art. III, Sec. 2's extension of federal judicial power "to controversies to which the United States shall be a party." But see Aetna Life Ins. Co. (U.S.1937).

§ 46-2. Federal "enclaves". A special problem of federal criminal jurisdiction, in the territorial sense, arises in respect of certain federal enclaves, as to which Congress may exercise exclusive jurisdiction. U. S. Constitution, Art. I, Sec. 8, Cl. 17. Contrast Carmen (N.D.Cal.1958), with Carmen (Cal.1957). Federal enclaves are geographical areas within a state but in which the federal government exercises general governmental powers. The general scheme is provided by the Assimilative Crimes Act, 18 U.S.C.A. § 13, whereby an act committed in such enclaves, which would be a crime by the law of the state in which it is located, is also a crime by federal law. Sharpnack (U.S.1958). Crimes committed on the *high seas,* other waters within the admiralty and maritime jurisdiction of the United States and out of state jurisdiction, and in other specified places, are also covered by 18 U.S.C.A. § 7. U. S. Constitution, Art. I, Sec. 8, Cl. 10 grants Congress power "To define and punish Piracies and Felonies committed on the high Seas, and Offenses against the Law of Nations," and Art. III, Sec. 2 extends the federal judicial power "to all Cases of admiralty and maritime Jurisdiction." Flores (U.S.1933).

§ 46–3. Venue. As venue of federal prosecutions, two provisions of the U. S. Constitution supply the starting point. Art. III, Sec. 2 provides: "The Trial of all Crimes, except in Cases of Impeachment, shall be by Jury; and such Trial shall be held in the State where the said Crimes shall have been committed; but when not committed within any State, the Trial shall be at such Place or Places as the Congress may by Law have directed." And the Sixth Amendment provides, in part: "In all criminal prosecutions, the accused shall enjoy the right to a speedy and public trial by an impartial jury of the State and district wherein the crimes shall have been committed, which district shall have been previously ascertained by law." These provisions reflect an ancient principle of the common law. It will be remembered that the Declaration of Independence itself criticized George III for combining with others "to subject us to a jurisdiction foreign to our constitution and unacknowledged by our laws" and complained that he was "transporting us beyond Seas to be tried for pretended offenses."

Fed.R.Crim.Proc. 18, as amended in 1966, states: "Except as otherwise permitted by statute or by these rules, the prosecution shall be had in a district in which the offense was committed. The court shall fix the place of trial within the district with due regard to the convenience of the defendant and the witnesses." 18 U.S.C.A. § 3238 provides that the "trial of all offenses begun or committed upon the high seas, or elsewhere out of the jurisdiction of any particular State or district, shall be in the district in which the offender . . . is arrested or is first brought." A number of statutes regulate particular proceedings, e. g. in respect to continuing offenses and offenses consisting of several transactions. Armour Packing Co. (U.S.1908), cf. Johnson (U.S. 1944). Although in criminal cases proper venue is a matter of constitutional right, it is a privilege of the defendant which is waived if he fails seasonably to object to improper venue. Hagner (C.A.D.C.1931).

D. Admiralty

§ 47–1. In general. The admiralty and maritime jurisdiction of the federal courts is a significant part of their business. Continuously since the Judiciary Act of 1789, Congress has effectuated its authority under the admiralty clause of Art. III, Sec. 2 of the Constitution by granting the federal courts such jurisdiction. But the effectuation has introduced exceptions to the "exclusive" nature of this "federal specialty." 28 U.S.C.A. § 1333 as now phrased provides that the district courts shall have original jurisdiction, exclusive of the courts of the states, of any civil admiralty or maritime case, "saving to suitors in all cases all other remedies to which they are otherwise entitled." Admiralty acts both in personam and in rem, and when the admiralty case is in rem, generally the federal jurisdiction is exclusive. But a plaintiff, known in admiralty practice as a libelant, may also prosecute his claim not only by an admiralty in personam action but, by reason of the "saving to suitors" clause, also by an action at law either in state court or federal court, if the requisites of federal jurisdiction are fulfilled. Romero (U.S.1959). On forum non conveniens and prorogation in admiralty, see §§ 17, 23.

§ 47-2. Bases of admiralty jurisdiction. The bases of federal admiralty jurisdiction are chiefly derived from concepts of ancient origin concerning the province of maritime law. With respect to torts, the traditional concept is that the place of the wrong determines whether the tort is governed by maritime law and is within admiralty jurisdiction. Thus, a tort occurring in or over navigable waters is within federal jurisdiction to adjudicate. The Plymouth (U.S.1860). Such a tort is also governed substantively by a federal "common law" of maritime torts developed in the federal courts. Guadet (U.S.1974).

With respect to contracts, the test for admiralty jurisdiction and governing law is not location but the character of the contract. If the contract is "maritime in nature," actions concerning obligations under the contract are within admiralty jurisdiction. The Moses Taylor (U.S.1867). If the contract is simply an incident to a maritime arrangement, however, it is not a maritime contract and admiralty jurisdiction does not exist. Thus, a contract covering a land-based warehouseman who received goods shipped by sea is not a maritime contract. Leather's Best (2d Cir. 1971).

In addition to the traditional bases of admiralty jurisdiction, Congress may by statute confer jurisdiction on admiralty courts in matters related to maritime commerce but not within the traditional scope of admiralty. Lindgren (U.S. 1930).

§ 47–3. Jury trial. The most significant difference between a case in admiralty and one at law is that the constitutional guarantee of *jury trial* is inapplicable to the former. However, Congress may provide for jury trial in admiralty even though the Constitution does not require it, as in the Jones Act, 46 U.S.C.A. Historically the procedural rules in admiralty cases had been separate and distinct from those in equity and law (merged in 1938 as "civil") actions. Miner (U.S.1960). But in 1966 unification of the civil and admiralty procedures was achieved. Fed.R.Civ. Proc. 1 now provides in part: "These rules govern the procedure in the United States district courts in all suits of a civil nature whether cognizable as cases at law or in equity or in admiralty." Supplemental Rules A, B, C, D, E and F were added to the civil rules for certain admiralty and maritime claims.

E. Other Special Jurisdictions

§ 48. The foregoing discussion of Government litigation, bankruptcy, criminal cases, and admiralty, should not mislead the student into thinking that all aspects of federal jurisdiction have been alluded to. A glance at U. S. Constitution, Art. III, should correct any such impression. We have not mentioned the original jurisdiction of the United States Supreme Court, e. g., in suits between states [28 U.S.C.A. § 1251; Texas v. Louisiana (U.S.1973)], or the appellate jurisdiction of the United States Courts of Appeals for the eleven circuits, and of the United States Supreme Court. See § 56. For discussion of Habeas Corpus see § 55. Such statutes as those regulating labor conditions or tort claims against the United States have, since the start of the Second World War, raised new jurisdictional problems in those foreign territories which, in varying ways and degrees, have been drawn into the political orbit of the United States.

2. SUBJECT MATTER JURISDICTION

§ 49. Introduction. The practice and procedure of the United States District Courts in civil cases are permeated by problems of jurisdiction similar to those affecting state courts. For example, the principle that actions for trespass to land are "local," i. e. jurisdictionally limited to the situs of the land, discussed in § 20, has been held applicable in federal court. Pasos (C.A.2, 1956 N.Y.); L & H 407. Again, since the amendment of Fed.R.Civ.Proc. 4(e) in 1963, the quasi in rem jurisdiction discussed in § 6, founded on garnishment, attachment or similar device, is possible in actions commenced in federal as in state courts. Prior to 1963, that kind of jurisdiction was available in federal court only in actions removed from state court. Rorick (U.S.1939); infra § 52.

But the federal courts under the Judiciary article of the Constitution of the United States, Art. III, are courts of specifically prescribed and hence limited jurisdiction. Hence, they have special jurisdictional problems.

A. Federal Claim

§ 50–1. The concept. The first of two broad classes of subject matter jurisdiction of the District Courts are cases "arising under" the United

States Constitution, laws and treaties. "Laws" of course includes federal statutes. The term has now been held also to include federal common law where there is such a body of doctrine, as with interstate aspects of water, for example, problems of pollution of a Great Lake. Illinois v. City of Milwaukee (U.S.1972); see § 53, infra. The concept "arising under" is an intricate one which has occasioned many decisions and much discussion. Osborn (U.S.1824). It means that the plaintiff's claim must seek to enforce a right of action conferred by the Constitution or laws. When a federal statute expressly confers a right of action, the claim clearly "arises under" federal law and is within the jurisdiction of the District Court. A more difficult problem is presented if the federal statute creates a duty on the part of a person but does not expressly provide that there shall be a right of action on the part of a person injured as a result of violation of that duty. This is the problem of an "implied" cause of action. If the statute is deemed to confer an implied right of action, plaintiff's claim is within federal jurisdiction. Cannon (U.S.1979). If not, plaintiff must sue on a common law theory in state court and rely on the federal statute as a standard of care or duty.

A similar problem is presented when plaintiff sues for injury resulting from violation of a Constitutional right. Some clauses of the Constitution have been deemed to create private rights of action. Bivens (U.S.1971). If so, the action is one that "arises under" the Constitution and is within the jurisdiction of the Federal District Court.

The federal basis of the suit (as distinguished from a common law or state statutory basis) must appear from the facts of the correctly pleaded complaint. It is not enough that a significant federal question—even one that might ultimately justify Supreme Court review—is involved by way of a defense.

Federal question jurisdiction is not exclusive except when federal law so provides. For example, actions under the anti-trust laws, 28 U.S.C. § 1337, are within the exclusive jurisdiction of the federal courts.

§ 50–2. "Pendent" jurisdiction. A plaintiff who has a claim "arising under" federal law may also have another claim concerning the same facts that is based on state law. For example, he may have a claim based on violation of the federal securities law and a claim based on the same transaction for fraud under state common law. The federal court may hear and decide the state claim in the course of the action. And it may give judgment for plaintiff on the state claim even though it finds against him on the merits of the federal claim. Jurisdiction over the state claim is called "pendent jurisdiction." Hurn (U.S.1933); J. I. Case (U.S.1964). A recent definition of "pendent" jurisdiction is: "The state and federal claims must derive from a common nucleus of operative fact. But if, considered without regard to their federal or state character, a plaintiff's claims are such that he would ordinarily be expected to try them all in one judicial proceeding, then, assuming substantiality of the federal issues, there is *power* in federal courts to hear the whole." United Mine Workers (U.S.1966).

Although the federal court has power to hear the state pendent claim, it is not required to do so. It may exercise discretion not to hear the state claim, remanding plaintiff to state court for its adjudication.

§ 50-3. "Ancillary" jurisdiction. Conceptually akin to "pendent" jurisdiction is "ancillary" jurisdiction. Indeed "ancillary jurisdiction" is now often called "pendent party" jurisdiction. The concept is that, once the federal court has jurisdiction of an action between two parties, it may consider other claims between them and also bring in other parties who have an interest in the original claim. The basic idea is that a federal court "acquires jurisdiction of a case or controversy as an entirety, and hence may, as an incident thereto, possess jurisdiction of matters [e. g. counter-claims, cross-claims, or claims of or against an impleaded party] of which it would not otherwise have cognizance were they independently presented." Yuba (C.A.9, 1953). It is under this concept that compulsory counterclaims, cross-claims, and impleader claims under Fed.R. Civ.Proc. 13 and 14 are supportable regardless of the citizenship of the parties, the amount in controversy, whether the claims arise under federal law, or any other factor that ordinarily would determine jurisdiction. For example, "ancillary" jurisdiction supports a compulsory counterclaim under Fed.R.Civ.Proc. 13(a), although apparently not a permissive one under Rule 13(b), regardless of the absence of other federal jurisdictional grounds. Great Lakes Rubber Corp. (C.A.3, 1961). Ancillary jurisdiction also supports claims in intervention of right under Rule 24(a).

However, attempts to expand ancillary jurisdiction have been discouraged by the Supreme Court. In Owen Equipment (U.S.1978) it held that ancillary jurisdiction would not permit a plaintiff to maintain an action against a co-defendant of an original defendant where the co-defendant was not of diverse citizenship from the plaintiff.

B. Diversity

§ 50–4. The concept. The second great branch of United States District Court original jurisdiction is diversity jurisdiction, usually concerned with suits between citizens of different states, but also encompassing suits between citizens of a state and foreign citizens. This normally requires complete diversity between all plaintiffs and all defendants; thus the presence of an indispensable defendant who is a co-citizen of any plaintiff defeats federal diversity jurisdiction. Strawbridge (U.S.1806). See § 27. The application of this rigid principle can cause dismissal of cases in federal court pursuant to the requirement of what is now Fed.R.Civ.Proc. 12(h)(3), that "Whenever it appears by suggestion of the parties or otherwise that the court lacks jurisdiction of the subject matter, the court shall dismiss the action." Calcote (C.A.5, 1946). Where necessary the court will realign parties as plaintiffs or defendants according to their true interests when passing on the compliance with the diversity requirement. Smith v. Sperling (U.S.1957).

The federal diversity jurisdiction is of course not exclusive; the appropriate state courts have concurrent jurisdiction. Therefore a plaintiff may elect to take his case to state court even though it fulfills all the requirements for federal diversity jurisdiction. But if he does elect a state court under such circumstances, the defendant has the option of removal to federal court, with certain limitations. See § 52.

§ 50–5. "Citizenship". For diversity purposes state citizenship means state domicile, i. e. permanent residence. Historically, a corporation in effect has been considered a citizen of the state of incorporation by reason of the conclusive presumption that all of its shareholders are citizens of such state. Louisville C. & Ch. R. R. (U.S. 1844). In 1958 Congress, in order to decrease diversity jurisdiction, added the qualification that a corporation is also a citizen "of the state where it has its principal place of business," 28 U.S.C.A. § 1332(c). Thus, a corporation incorporated in Delaware and having its principal place of business is, for diversity purposes, a citizen of both Delaware and New York. It follows that such a corporation could not be an adversary in a diversity case of *either* a citizen of Delaware *or* New York.

An unincorporated association, as well as a partnership, is regarded as having citizenship in every state in which any of its individual members are citizens. Thus an unincorporated political organization or union having members who are citizens of States X, Y, and Z is, for diversity purposes, a citizen of all those states.

When the suit is by a representative party, it is the representative's citizenship that counts in determining whether there is diversity. Thus, if T is killed in an accident with D, and A is thereafter appointed T's administrator, for diversity purposes the question is whether A and D are citizens of different states. However, this rule is subject to the qualification that the person selected as administrator must have some reason for being so other than the fact of diverse citizenship from the tortfeasor; if he was chosen solely to create diversity the court will look to the decedent's citizenship to determine whether there is diversity jurisdiction. McSparran (3d Cir. 1968).

§ 50–6. Interpleader. An important exception to the requirement of complete diversity (as well as to normally applicable venue and jurisdictional amount requirements) is afforded by Federal Statutory Interpleader. By reason of 28 U.S.C.A. § 1335 the diversity requirements are satisfied as to such cases whenever "two or more adverse claimants, of diverse citizenship" make claim to property. State Farm (U.S.1967). This is not to be confused with interpleader under Fed.R.Civ. Proc. 22, which requires diversity between plaintiff stakeholder and all other parties and also requires compliance with all other normally applicable conditions of federal jurisdiction.

C. Limitations

§ 51–1. Amount. The general "federal question" jurisdiction, 28 U.S.C.A. § 1331, and the diversity jurisdiction, 28 U.S.C.A. § 1332, both require the "matter in controversy" exceeds, exclusive of interest and costs, $10,000. Some of the specific grants of federal jurisdiction have different minima, e. g. Federal Statutory Interpleader has $500 [28 U.S.C.A. § 1335], and some have none at all, e. g. 28 U.S.C.A. § 1337 (actions based on federal statutes regulating commerce) and 1343 (actions based on violation of Constitutional rights or statutes protecting equal rights).

An important corollary in connection with the amount in controversy requirement is the rule limiting aggregation of claims. A single plaintiff, or multiple plaintiffs having a joint interest in the claims, may add up all claims in his complaint against defendant for purposes of determining whether the $10,000 minimum has been met. Thus, if P has two wholly separate claims against D, but the total value of the claims exceeds $10,000, the requirement is met. However, multiple parties may not aggregate their claims. Thus, if H and W are both injured in an automobile accident with D, and H's claim is for $15,000 and W's for $2,000, W may not be joined with H in a federal court action against D. This is because W's claim considered alone would not meet the amount in controversy minimum and cannot be aggregated with—that is, added to—H's claim. This holds even if they were husband and wife or otherwise related. The same principle prevents members of a class whose claims are each less than $10,000 from aggregating their claims to achieve federal jurisdiction. Zahn (U. S.1974).

§ 51–2. Service of process. Normally service of process for in personam actions, whether within the federal question or diversity jurisdiction, is restricted to the territorial limits of the state in which the United States District Court is held. Fed.R.Civ.Proc. 4(f). Where constructive service is possible under state "long-arm" statutes (§§ 4, 5), federal courts follow the practice of the state in which they sit. Since 1963 they must do so also in "quasi in rem" cases where jurisdiction is founded on garnishment or attachment. Fed.R. Civ.Proc. 4(e); supra § 6. A number of federal statutes have special provisions for nationwide service of process in particular types of actions created by those statutes.

§ 51–3. Venue. Where jurisdiction is founded solely on diversity of citizenship, the only correct venue is the judicial district where all plaintiffs or all defendants reside or the district in which the claim arose. In all other cases (and hence in "federal question" cases), normally the correct venue is the judicial district where all defendants reside or the district in which the claim arose. 28 U.S.C.A. § 1391(a), (b). But particular statutes may provide a different venue, e. g. a Federal Statutory Interpleader action may be brought in the judicial district "in which one or more of the claimants reside." 28 U.S.C.A. § 1397. For venue purposes, a defendant corporation is a resident of each judicial district in which it is incorporated or licensed to do business or is doing business. 28 U.S.C.A. § 1391(c). But this applies only to corporate defendants and does not for venue purposes make a plaintiff corporation a resident of the district in which it is doing business. Manchester Modes (C.A.2d 1970). Aliens are suable in any district. Brunette (U.S.1972). Improper venue seasonably objected to will require dismissal or transfer; under 28 U.S.C.A. § 1406(a), if venue is improper but there is a district in which the action might properly have been brought, the court may transfer venue to that district. Compare § 17.

§ 51–4. Forum non conveniens. Since the enactment in 1948 of the provision that for the convenience of parties and witnesses, in the interest of justice, the "district court may transfer any civil action to any other district or division where it might have been brought," 28 U.S.C.A. § 1404(a), normally the remedy for plaintiff's selection of an inconvenient forum is transfer to an appropriate district. Norwood (U.S.1955); Van Dusen (U.S.1964). As noted at the beginning of this section, the local action rule concerned with actions for trespass to land, discussed in § 20 supra, is applicable in federal court.

§ 51–5. Abstention. In recent times the United States Supreme Court has buttressed an additional "hurdle" to the exercise of federal jurisdiction, namely the abstention doctrine. Roughly, its philosophy is that federal district courts in certain kinds of cases should withhold their jurisdiction pending decision of potentially controlling state issues by the state court. Railroad Comm'n (U.S.1941); Trainor (U.S.1977). Some applications of the doctrine have evoked cogent dissents. Clay (U.S.1960). And see England (U.S.1964). The effect of the pendency of actions in other courts was discussed in § 18.

3. REMOVAL JURISDICTION

§ 52. Sometimes an action which has all of the requisites for original jurisdiction (either "federal question" or diversity) in federal court, is nevertheless brought in a state court simply because the plaintiff elects the state court. (We speak now of cases of which federal and state courts have concurrent jurisdiction. See § 50–1). Such an action may be removed upon demand of the defendants from the state court to the federal district court embracing the place where the action is pending. 28 U.S.C.A. § 1441(a).

"Federal-question" cases are removable without regard to the citizenship of the parties. Diversity cases are removable only if none of the defendants is a citizen of the state in which the action is brought. 28 U.S.C.A. § 1441(b); American Fire & Cas. (U.S.1951). Sometimes, however, a statute expressly prohibits removal of cases otherwise removable, e. g. in F.E.L.A. cases. And for some kinds of cases there are special provisions, e. g. for civil rights cases, 28 U.S.C.A. § 1443, and suits against federal officers, 28 U.S.C.A. § 1442.

To illustrate the general removal statute, 28 U.S.C.A. § 1441, assume that a New Yorker assaults a Californian, inflicting more than $10,000 damages. The Californian may bring an in personam action in the United States District Court in New York in the district of defendant's residence; there is diversity of citizenship and the requisite amount; service presumably may be made personally as defendant is a New York resident; the New York venue is appropriate. If the Californian were content to sue in an appropriate New York state court, the New Yorker could not remove to federal court because of the diversity case rule against removal by a resident. 28 U.S.C.A. § 1441(b). If the Californian caught the New Yorker with service of process in California, the action could be maintained there in federal court because the residence of plaintiff is also a correct venue in diversity cases. But if the Californian sued instead in a California state court, the New Yorker could remove to federal court because he is a nonresident. Where removal is proper, the appropriate venue on removal is "the district and division embracing the place where such action is pending in state court." 28 U.S.C.A. § 1441(a).

The removal jurisdiction is said to be strictly derivative. Where plaintiff commences in state court an action of a kind within the exclusive jurisdiction of a federal court, e. g. a patent case, and an attempt is thereafter made to remove to the federal court, the case must there be dismissed: Although it could, and indeed should, originally have been commenced in federal court, there was no state jurisdiction from which federal jurisdiction could be derived. See American Well Works (U.S.1916).

4. THE ERIE PROBLEM

§ 53–1. From Swift to Erie. When a federal court adjudicates a claim, what law does it employ? To the extent the case is governed by federal law—Constitution, statute, treaty, and their interpretation—clearly that law is applied. But if no federal provision is dispositive, the question is whether the federal courts should apply the law of the state or should fashion their own idea of the law. This is the *Erie* problem.

The first Congress enacted the Rules of Decision Act (Judiciary Act of 1789, § 34, 1 Stat. 92) which, as phrased today, provides that "The laws of the several states, except where the Constitution or treaties of the United States or Acts of

Congress otherwise require or provide, shall be regarded as rules of decision in civil actions in the courts of the United States, in cases where they apply." 28 U.S.C.A. § 1652. Under Swift (U.S.1842) and its progeny, the mandate of that Act was restricted to state statutes and other "local" matters, so that on matters of "general federal common law," including commercial law and torts, the federal courts, even in diversity cases, pursued freely their own jurisprudence uninhibited by state decisions, not hesitating to depart from the precedents of the highest courts of the states in which they sat. This practice crested in Black & White Taxicab Co. (U.S.1928). In that case, by the artifice of dissolving and reincorporating in a different state so as to create diversity in relation to its opponent, a corporation was able to get from a federal judge an injunction which state law would have denied as violative of its policy against restraints of trade. The Black & White case, jurisprudentially offensive as it was, nevertheless was only one of numerous situations wherein a party, by the accident of diversity, could obtain a result in federal court different from that which would ensue in a state court in the absence of diversity. Thus was focused up the anomaly whereby bifurcated judicial administration in the same territory produced differing —sometimes diametrically opposed—substantive results.

The Supreme Court sought to end this anomaly in Erie (U.S.1938). According to that case, the Rules of Decision Act was merely declaratory of the constitutional obligation of the federal courts to follow state substantive law on nonfederal issues. Thus, by applying the rule of Swift v. Tyson, federal courts had taken the constitutionally impermissible course of construing the Rules of Decision Act too narrowly. Although this constitutional rationale of the Erie doctrine is limited to diversity suits, its total operative scope is not so limited. For the dichotomy effected by the Rules of Decision Act is not between diversity and federal-question litigation, but between cases where the United States Constitution, treaties or laws apply, on the one hand, and those where they do not apply, on the other. Thus state law may apply under that Act even in "federal-question" litigation insofar as particular issues involved are not governed by federal law. Wichita Royalty (U.S.1939). On the other hand even in diversity cases, issues sometimes arise which are controlled by federal law so that a federal court must resolve them unfettered by Erie [Francis (U.S.1948) (interpretation of federal statute)] just as a state court must follow federal rather than state precedents on federal issues. Dice (U.S.1952).

But state law can be displaced by "federal common law" in limited areas. These are areas of federal activity where federal statute does not provide the governing rule but where a uniform federal provision is thought desirable. Such a rule is fashioned through judicial decision—hence "federal common law."

Areas of "federal common law" include aspects of federal financial operations, Clearfield Trust (U.S.1943) and labor relations affecting interstate commerce, Textile Workers (U.S.1957). But cf. De Sylva (U.S.1956) (meaning of "children" in the Copyright Act). And of course Congress explicitly may adopt state law, as it has in the Federal Tort Claims Act, 28 U.S.C.A. § 1346(b), and with regard to certain aspects of federal tax law.

The *Erie* doctrine requires that federal courts apply state rules as to choice of law. Klaxon (U.S.1941); Day and Zimmerman (U.S.1975).

§ 53-2. Substance or procedure: outcome? How comprehensive is the Erie mandate to follow "[t]he laws of the several states?" The basic distinction is between "substance" and "procedure." Paradoxically, the year 1938 in which Erie was decided was also the year in which the Federal Rules of Civil Procedure, promulgated by the United States Supreme Court, became effective. The Congressional Enabling Act authorized the Court to prescribe rules for the "practice and procedure" of the district courts, but included the limitation that the rules "shall not abridge, enlarge or modify any substantive right." 28 U.S.C.A. § 2072. The Enabling Act and Rules superseded the old Conformity Act, 17 Stat. 197, under which the practice of the federal district courts in suits at law conformed, as nearly as feasible, to the practice of the courts of the state in which the federal court was held. (For equity and admiralty cases, the federal district courts long had followed separate procedural rules promulgated by the Supreme Court). The Federal Rules of Civil Procedure in 1938 merged law and equity cases into one form of civil action, and in 1966 admiralty cases were added, Rule 1, so that the Rules now govern all matters of "procedure" in all suits of a civil nature with certain stated exceptions. Rule 81.

The question of how "procedure" is to be distinguished from "substantive right" is thus pertinent both from the viewpoint of Erie's constitutional mandate in diversity cases and of the Enabling Act's limitation in all cases. Sibbach (U.S. 1941). A classic attempt to draw the line, for Erie purposes, was that of Frankfurter, J. in Guaranty Trust (U.S.1945): a rule of law is within Erie's mandate if it has a substantial effect on the outcome of the case. Under this test federal courts were compelled to abide state law with regard to questions which for other purposes are often treated as procedural, such as the requirement of security for stockholders' derivative suits [Cohen (U.S.1949)], the statute of limitations [Guaranty Trust, supra], the commencement of law suits for purposes of tolling statutes of limitations [Ragan (U.S.1949)], and exclusion of nonqualified foreign corporations [Woods (U.S.1949)]. Even before Guaranty Trust, Erie's mandate had been applied to burden of proof in a suit to quiet title [Cities Service Oil (U.S.1939)], burden of proof as to contributory negligence [Palmer (U.S.1943)], and the state's conflict of laws rule [Klaxon (U.S.1941)].

§ 53–3. Impinging federal values. The Guaranty Trust case's "outcome" test for Erie's applicability held sway in the Supreme Court for about thirteen years. But it proved too much, for rules of procedure, as well as rules of substantive law, affect "outcome". If rules conventionally classifiable as "procedural" had to be subordinated to state requirements when they affect or might affect outcome, clearly many of the Federal Rules of Civil Procedure would have to give way to conflicting state statutes or rules. Also, there were federal procedural rules that were prescribed by the Constitution, notably the right to jury trial.

In 1958 an issue arose as to whether an injured workman was a statutory employee of the alleged tortfeasor. If so, his remedy was exclusively under the workmen's compensation law; if not, he was free to sue at common law for negligence. In state court that issue would have been decided by the judge. Should a federal court in a diversity suit follow the state mode of trial under Erie or accord jury trial of the issue under the Seventh Amendment? The Supreme Court conceded that, if "outcome" were the only consideration, a strong case might appear for following state practice. But it held that the preference under the Seventh Amendment for jury trial of disputed fact questions countervailed against and superseded the otherwise applicable Erie obligation to follow the state practice. Byrd (U.S.1958); see also Simler (U.S.1963).

The qualification of the "outcome" test continued apace in Hanna (U.S.1965). There an Ohio citizen sued the Massachusetts executor of the deceased Massachusetts tortfeasor in federal court in the latter state. Abode service was made on defendant under Federal Rules of Civil Procedure 4(d)(1), by leaving a copy of the summons at his home with his wife. But the Massachusetts statute required delivery in hand to defendant because he was an executor. Defendant's motion for summary judgment on the ground of inadequate service was granted by the district court, citing Guaranty Trust. The Supreme Court, per Warren, C. J., reversed, holding that Rule 4(d)(1) controlled. It held that the Rule was within the scope of the Enabling Act as prescribing "practice and procedure" and does not abridge any "substantive" right, citing Sibbach (U.S.1941). The Court additionally stated that, even if there were no Federal Rule of Civil Procedure making it clear that in-hand service is not required in diversity actions, it is doubtful that the outcome test of the Guaranty Trust case would require application of state law. The Court conceded that application of the Massachusetts statute would be "outcome-determinative" because the statute of limitations now prevented plaintiff from recommencing the suit with in-hand service. Nevertheless, the Court said that the difference between the state and federal rules for service of process would have scant relevance to the original choice of a forum, so that the underlying philosophy of the Guaranty Trust outcome test, namely, the discouragement of forum shopping and avoidance of inequitable administration of the laws, was not violated by refusing to follow the state method of service. In any event, Rule 4(d)(1) does not exceed the constitutional bounds underlying Erie; the constitutional provision for a federal court system carries with it congressional power to make rules governing the practice and pleading in federal courts. Harlan, J., while agreeing with the judgment of the Court, criticized what he regarded as its "arguably procedural, *ergo* constitutional" rationale to protect the paramountcy of the Federal Rules over conflicting state rules. For him, the proper line of approach to determine whether an issue is "substantive," hence controlled by Erie, or "procedural," hence controlled by the Federal Rules, is to inquire "if the choice of rule would substantially affect those primary decisions respecting human conduct which our constitutional system leaves to state regulation." Id. at 475, 85 S.Ct. at 1146. Following Hanna, a dispute arose and continues as to whether it overrules the Ragan decision to follow state law in determining when a suit commences. Compare, e. g., Lindsey (10th Cir. 1979) (Ragan still good law), with Ingram (2d Cir. 1978) (Ragan overruled by Hanna).

Hanna has clearly shifted the line of division between state and federal law from its location under Guaranty Trust. But drawing the line remains an ambiguous undertaking. For example, in Woods (5th Cir. 1979) plaintiff allegedly suffered medical malpractice in Florida. Florida statute requires that a medical malpractice claimant submit the claim to a mediation panel before bringing suit. The panel's decision is then admissible in evidence if the claim is not settled. In plaintiff's malpractice action in federal court on diversity jurisdiction, held, submission to mediation was a condition precedent applicable in federal court as in state court. The court rejected contentions that the state statute was "merely procedural" and that its operation would interfere with the federal jury trial right.

In Britt (3d Cir. 1978), the plaintiff sued in federal court, naming one defendant as "John Doe." Through discovery the true name was ascertained and summons and complaint were served on the real person so identified. Under state law the complaint would relate back so as not to be barred by the statute of limitations. Under F.R. C.P. 15 it would not relate back. Held: No relation back, for the matter is governed by the Federal Rules.

5. FEDERAL JURISDICTION TOMORROW

§ 54. In the United States we maintain two separate hierarchies of courts, state and federal. This contrasts for example with the Canadian federalism which knows no Dominion trial courts with jurisdiction analogous to that of our United States District Courts. Our system has obvious advantages from the viewpoint of maintaining a strong and independent federal government. Still, although we incur the expense of two separate court systems, not infrequently, aggrieved persons are effectively barred from judicial redress, even in federal court, by a combination of the "hurdles" to jurisdiction discussed above. Thus a plaintiff may be unable to serve all necessary defendants within the borders of a particular state or, again, even if he is lucky enough to catch them all there, it may be an inappropriate venue with relief under 28 U.S.C.A. § 1404(a) not available. Hoffman (U.S.1960).

Thus, even with two elaborate judicial systems, justice may fail because of jurisdictional limitations. The minimum remedy would seem to be *nationwide service* of process in federal courts in cases where the plaintiff cannot otherwise get jurisdiction over all of the requisite defendants. It is believed that a step down the right road was taken by the 1963 amendment to Fed.R.Civ.Proc. 4(f), permitting service in certain cases "at all places outside the state but within the United States that are not more than 100 miles from the place in which the action is commenced, or to which it is assigned or transferred for trial."

Today most lawyers assume that the "federal question" jurisdiction is of the essence of a federal system like ours, once the decision has been taken to maintain a system of federal courts independent of those of the states. The current emphasis of the prestigious American Law Institute is to expand and strengthen this branch of jurisdiction because "[F]ederal question jurisdiction is necessary to preserve uniformity in federal law and to protect litigants relying on federal law from the danger that state courts will not properly apply that law, either through misunderstanding or lack of sympathy." The American Law Institute, Study of the Division of Jurisdiction between State and Federal Courts, Tentative Draft No. 5 at 1 (1967). The expansion would be achieved principally by permitting removal from state to federal court on the basis of a federal defense or counterclaim (in addition to the removal now permitted when the federal question appears on the face of the well-pleaded complaint, § 50). Study, supra (1969) 25–26. Further the requirement that there be a specified minimum amount in controversy (now $10,000; § 51) would be abandoned in the case of a federal claim or counterclaim. Id. at 26. Liberalizing venue provisions and permission for nationwide service of process would also be added. Id. at 30–31. A good resume of the reform proposals before Congress as this edition goes to press appears in Hearings before the Subcommittee of the Committee on the Judiciary, U. S. Senate, S. 1876, p. 1 (Part 1, 1971).

But what of the necessity for and the wisdom of *diversity* jurisdiction, dependent as it is not on conventional subject matter but on the citizenship of the parties? Does it make sense to maintain for rights of recovery derived not from the United States but from one of the states, a duplicate or concurrent jurisdiction when the federal court under the doctrine of Erie v. Tompkins must decide the substantive issues of the case under the law of the state in which it sits? In the words of Frankfurter, J., does this not make "a federal court adjudicating a state-created right solely because of the diversity of citizenship of the parties . . . for that purpose, in effect, only another court of the State"? Guaranty Trust (U.S.1945). Certain it is that the authority for the diversity jurisdiction contained in U. S. Constitution, Art. III is not self-executing; Congress is free to curtail or wholly abolish that jurisdiction at will. [It is indeed theoretically free from the constitutional viewpoint generally to abolish all of the jurisdiction of the United States District Courts, and the appellate jurisdiction of the Supreme Court; though it cannot modify the latter's original jurisdiction. Marbury (U.S.1803)]. Should Congress curtail or abolish the diversity jurisdiction?

Doubtless the assumed justification for the diversity jurisdiction—the potential prejudice of state courts against "foreigners"—is not verifiable in any sense that approaches scientific certainty. Nevertheless the real need seems to be enlargement of the diversity jurisdiction by means of nationwide service of process for those cases wherein no state can obtain jurisdiction of all necessary parties. The American Law Institute has recognized this in proposing, with accordant auxiliary provisions, that the federal district courts "shall have original jurisdiction of any civil action in which the several defendants who are necessary for a just adjudication of the plaintiff's claim are not all amenable to process of any one territorial jurisdiction, and one of any two adverse parties is a citizen of a State and the other is a citizen or subject of another territorial jurisdiction." Study, supra (1969) 67. Liberalizing provisions in respect of venue and service of process nationwide, and beyond, are also recommended. Id. at 69, 72. See Hearings before the Subcommittee, supra, p. 1.

HABEAS CORPUS

§ 55–1. Concept. Habeas corpus, Anglo-American society's ultimate, and perhaps chief, guarantee of personal freedom, known as the "Great Writ" [Bollman (U.S.1807); Fay (U.S. 1963)], seems generally to fall into a no-man's land so far as writers on jurisdiction are concerned, as indeed it does in law school curricula. Possibly this is because, while analytically a civil proceeding, it often pertains to criminal matters—although not always so, as witness its use in child custody cases. May (U.S.1953).

The chief purpose of the writ of habeas corpus is to give a person restrained of his liberty an immediate hearing to determine the legality of his detention. The writ is directed by the judge to the person exercising the detention, commanding the production in open court of the body of the subject. This production of the body in court is unique to the Great Writ, ensuring a confrontation between the one detained and his detainor and a full exploration before the court of the issues, historically jurisdictional but increasingly substantive, concerning the detention.

The fundamental significance of the writ of habeas corpus in our society is shown by the fact that, as respects the federal government, it enjoys constitutional status. U. S. Constitution, Art. I, Sec. 9 provides: "The Privilege of the Writ of Habeas Corpus shall not be suspended, unless when in Cases of Rebellion or Invasion the public Safety may require it." Indeed, the power to issue writs of habeas corpus has been called "the loftiest power with which the Constitution has endowed" the federal courts. Johnson (U.S. 1950). In order to ensure the fullest scope to this power, the Supreme Court has relieved the operation of the writ from several restrictions. The doctrine of res judicata has been held inapplicable [Sanders (U.S.1963)] and pleading requirements have been liberalized [Price (U.S. 1948)]. Further, the requirement of a full factual hearing has been reinforced [Townsend (U. S.1963)].

Habeas corpus is no less significant in state practice. Commonly not only trial court judges of courts with plenary jurisdiction, but appellate judges also, have power to issue the writ. Thus 28 U.S.C.A. § 2241(a) states that "Writs of habeas corpus may be granted by the Supreme Court, any justice thereof, the district courts and any circuit judge within their respective jurisdictions." But either by statute or rule, normally the writ is first to be sought from a competent judge on the lowest level of the judicial hierarchy, unless a sufficient showing is made to justify application in the first instance to a higher judge or court.

§ 55–2. Scope. The United States Supreme Court long took the position, over strong dissent, that "[T]he words 'within their respective jurisdictions' limit the district courts to inquiries into the causes of restraints of liberty of those confined or restrained within the territorial jurisdictions of those courts." It was not sufficient that the jailor or custodian alone was found in the jurisdiction. Ahrens (U.S.1948); cf. Ex parte Endo (U.S.1944); Jones (U.S.1963). But a viewpoint more accordant with the purposes and significance of the Great Writ, yet feasible administratively at least for the states, was expressed by Judge Cooley in Jackson (Mich.1867): "The important fact to be observed in regard to the mode of procedure upon this writ is that it is directed to, and served upon, not the person confined, but his jailor. It does not reach the former except through the latter. The officer or person who serves it does not unbar the prison doors, and set the prisoner free, but the court relieves him by compelling the oppressor to release his constraint. The whole force of the writ is spent upon the respondent . . .. The place of confinement is, therefore, not important to the relief, if the guilty party is within reach of process, so that by the power of the court he can be compelled to release his grasp. The difficulty of affording redress is not increased by the confinement being beyond the limits of the state, except as greater distance may affect it. The important question is, where is the power of control exercised?" And the Court in Braden (U.S.1973) approvingly quoted Judge Cooley's language in holding that petitioner, imprisoned in Alabama, could apply to the Kentucky federal court for habeas corpus to compel Kentucky to grant him a speedy trial on a charge pending there.

In addition to the jurisdictional problem mentioned above, another problem often cast in "jurisdictional" terminology concerns the reach or remediable scope of habeas corpus. Should it be available to relieve from confinement only those whose commitment was jurisdictionally void, or also the victims of serious error which does not "go to" jurisdiction in the classic sense but may effect a deprivation of constitutional right, e. g. right to counsel? Johnson (U.S.1938). In Waley

(U.S.1942), the Court said that habeas corpus in federal courts is not restricted to cases where the judgment of conviction is jurisdictionally void but "extends also to those exceptional cases where the conviction has been in disregard of the constitutional rights of the accused, and where the writ is the only effective means of preserving his rights." More recently, the availability of the writ in such circumstances is simply assumed. Roberts (U.S.1968); cf. Nelson (U.S.1971).

The writ can be available in unusual circumstances as a remedy in a civil case. Cases of child custody are one example. Another is as relief from imprisonment for civil contempt under state court process. Morgan (5th Cir. 1971).

APPELLATE JURISDICTION

§ 56-1. History and comparison. Concepts rooted in jurisdictional limitations continue to flourish in American appellate practice, state and federal. Typically in continental countries the "appeal," that is, a proceeding of second instance, is a continuation of the first instance proceeding insofar as it offers the possibility of introducing additional evidence. In England all appeals are by way of rehearing of trial court processes and hence analogous to historic equity review. But American appellate practice essentially is in successorship to writ of error review which was review of a record rather than a case.

§ 56–2. Timeliness. The validity of the process of taking an appeal is typically dependent upon the timely filing of a notice of appeal and lodgment of the record in the appellate court. These steps, especially the first, often are conceived of as "jurisdictional" in the sense that failure of timely performance may invalidate the appeal and the lapse of the prescribed period may render the appellant remediless. The logic is a vestige of writ of error practice whereby the process of obtaining review constituted a new proceeding and had to conform to jurisdictional requisites. This results in the United States in the dismissal of many appeals without any consideration of the merits. Occasionally a court has power to extend the time within which to perform a jurisdictional act, but it may be essential that the extension be obtained prior to expiration of the originally prescribed period. Thus, a Justice of the United States Supreme Court, for good cause shown, may extend the ordinarily applicable ninety-days period (from the entry of judgment below) in which to apply for certiorari for a period not exceeding sixty days. 28 U.S.C.A. § 2101(c). But the application for extension must be presented "within the period sought to be extended." U.S. Supreme Court Rule 34–2. The problem of filing the notice of appeal within the prescribed period from the entry of the judgment appealed from may be compounded by ambiguity in the applicable statute or rule as to when judgment is entered. F. & M. Schaefer (U.S.1958); see Fed.R.Civ.Proc. 58, 79(a). True, in federal appellate practice a reading of a notice of appeal so narrowly as effectively to preclude review, was reproved [Foman (U.S.1962)], but the cautious student will limit such cases to their precise holding.

Even the foregoing brief paragraph should make obvious to the student that American appellate practice presents many "jurisdictional" pitfalls and that any failure of alertness or diligence by counsel can cause the loss forever of a client's right to obtain appellate review of the merits. Louisell and Degnan, Rehearing in American Appellate Courts, 44 Calif.L.Rev. 627 (1956); 34 Can.Bar Review 898 (1956); 25 Fed. R.Dec. 143 (1960).

§ 56-3. Finality rule. One of the most universal and fundamental concepts of American appellate practice is that, express exceptions aside, only a final judgment is appealable. Cobbledick (U.S.1940). In federal appellate practice, the express statutory exceptions are interlocutory injunction and receivership orders, admiralty decrees, patent infringement judgments final except for accounting, 28 U.S.C.A. § 1292, and certain bankruptcy orders, e. g. 11 U.S.C.A. Also, 28 U.S.C.A. § 1292(b), enacted in 1958, grants discretion to the courts of appeals to review any interlocutory order if the trial judge states in writing that the "order involves a controlling question of law as to which there is substantial ground for difference of opinion and that an immediate appeal may materially advance the ultimate termination of the litigation." Further, an appeal as to fewer than all the claims or by fewer than all the parties is possible where the trial court expressly determines according to Fed.R.Civ.Proc. 54 (b) that there is "no just reason for delay" and so directs the entry of judgment. And there are a few judicially created exceptions to the finality rule to overcome its felt deficiencies. E. g., Forgay (U.S.1848) (orders not absolutely final may nevertheless be appealable if otherwise the losing parties would be subjected to irreparable injury); Cohen (U.S.1949) (disposition of a collateral right may be appealable without awaiting the final judgment); Cox (U.S.1975) (appealability to U. S. Supreme Court of nonfinal judgment in state court).

§ 56–4. Extraordinary writs. Of the four *extraordinary writs,* quo warranto, certiorari, mandamus and prohibition, the last three often are used in effect to perform an appellate function, especially in situations where the trial court's action is regarded as so egregiously erroneous as to be characterizable as beyond its "jurisdiction." (Such use is of course to be distinguished from use to obtain judicial review of administrative action, an important concern of Administrative Law.) Thus, mandamus has been used to correct a trial judge's erroneous reference of a case to a master where an appeal was not possible because there was as yet no final judgment [La Buy (U. S.1957)], and to correct his erroneous order for acquittal in a criminal case where otherwise the government would have been remediless because it cannot appeal from a judgment of acquittal. United States (C.A.1, 1961) (though retrial would violate the Fifth Amendment's guaranty that no person shall "be subject for the same offense to be twice put in jeopardy of life or limb," and mandamus therefore should not have issued, the Court did not criticize the use of mandamus, procedurally, to raise the issue).

Sometimes, as in California, mandamus and prohibition have evolved on a case to case basis as the most suitable and convenient techniques for reviewing, prior to final judgment, a trial court's discovery orders. Oceanside (Cal.1962); Louisell & Wally, Modern California Discovery §§ 1.04, 2.10 (2d ed. 1972). And there is indication that, at least where the question is regarded as of fundamental importance, the federal courts may follow suit under the "All-Writs" statute, 28 U.S.

C.A. § 1651. Atlass (C.A.7, 1959); Schlagenhauf (U.S.1964). Moreover, the California legislature explicitly has specified mandamus as the appropriate device for prompt appellate review of orders denying motions to quash service of summons upon the ground of lack of jurisdiction. Cal.Code Civ.Proc. § 418.10; Hartford (Cal. 1956). Perhaps the extraordinary writs will develop as expeditious tools for review of orders erroneously denying relief under forum non conveniens. Cf. Parsons (U.S.1963) (railway company not entitled in federal court to mandamus to compel a transfer under 28 U.S.C.A. § 1404(a), as the state court's prior holding of forum non conveniens did not bind the federal judge; but mandamus was assumed, procedurally, to be the proper way to raise the question). See also La Buy (U. S.1957).

JURISDICTION REVISITED: FORUM CONVENIENS

THE NUTSHELL "IN A NUTSHELL"

§ 57. 1. *Personal jurisdiction* over corporations, other associations and individuals may be constitutionally obtained in compliance with a statute of the state

a. by personal service of process within that state (§ 3) or consent (§§ 4–1, 4–2, 4–3, 4–4);

b. by constructive service (personal service outside the state, publication, service through the mail or statutory agents) combined with prescribed direct notification: if the defendant is domiciled in the state (§§ 4–6, 4–7) or if "fair play and substantial justice" are otherwise secured through "minimum contacts" with the state (§ 4–13) such as commission of a tortious act (§§ 4–5, 4–12, 5–4, 5–5, 5–6, 5–7, 5–8), ownership of the damaging property (§ 4–9), or continuous and systematic activities at the time of the accrual of the cause of action (§§ 4–8, 4–14, 5–2, 5–3).

2. *Attachment jurisdiction* may be acquired by constructive service where defendant's property has been brought under the control of the court and where the forum has "minimum contacts" with the case. § 6. The purpose of such an action is to apply the property to payment of plaintiff's claim.

3. *Jurisdiction in rem* over a res located within the state may be obtained by constructive service combined with an attempt at giving the defendant fair notice. § 7. The purpose of such an action is to determine claims of interest in the property itself. One of the most important applications of this rule concerns the law of *divorce* in

which the petitioner's domicile is treated as the location of the marriage res. Through the doctrine of "participation", however, divorce jurisdiction has acquired important attributes of personal jurisdiction (§§ 8–1, 8–2, 8–3). Similar developments have occurred in the laws of annulment (§ 11) and decedents' estates (§ 15).

4. In certain *domestic relations* involving children (including support, custody and adoption), traditional categories of jurisdiction are replaced by a flexible regime designed to serve primarily the child's welfare. §§ 11–13.

5. In the federal courts and in about one-half of the states a suit may be dismissed (and in the federal courts transferred to a more appropriate court) for reasons of fairness to the defendant and other reasons of "convenience." Other specific instances of discretionary dismissals (other actions pending, internal corporate affairs) are likely to merge in this doctrine of *forum non conveniens*. §§ 15–16.

6. Jurisdiction otherwise available may be *excluded* by the common law (local action) (§ 20), the Constitution (full faith and credit and interstate commerce) (§§ 21–22), or party agreement (prorogation and arbitration) (§§ 23, 24).

7. Suits may also be dismissed on "*quasi-jurisdictional*" grounds, including lack of procedural capacity (standing to sue and to be sued), run-

ning of the statute of limitations, res judicata, extinction of the claim by a party's death, and violation of public policy. These grounds are sometimes said "to go to the jurisdiction," because, without affecting the merits of the claim, they may permanently preclude its enforcement. §§ 25–35.

8. Notwithstanding the court's (local) jurisdiction and its ability and willingness to take such jurisdiction, suit may be inexpedient because the judgment thus obtained would lack the *interstate* or *international jurisdiction* required by the state of presumable enforcement or other recognition. Although interstate jurisdiction for purposes of full faith and credit will usually coincide with local jurisdiction under due process, the laws of divorce and probate offer crucial examples for possible divergencies. §§ 15, 36–40.

9. The requirement of proper *venue* normally is not jurisdictional since it is waivable by defendant. An exception is that certain actions concerning realty must be brought in the county where the land or a portion of it is located. § 43.

10. *Criminal jurisdiction* is typically limited to crimes committed in the court's territory. But this principle is losing some of its rigidity by the recognition of jurisdictions based on allegiance and the forum's security interest, and the broadening of the crime's localization. § 41. On the

other hand, the concept of a "personal" jurisdiction limited to persons before the court has been preserved at least as to major crimes though its effect has been weakened by resort to international and interstate extradition. § 42.

11. Certain problems of *federal "jurisdiction"* are identical with or similar to the jurisdictional problems of the states. The limitation for most lawsuits of service of process to the territorial limits of the state in which the federal district court is held, and the obeisance of federal courts to the local action rule, are illustrative. But the additional problems of "federal jurisdiction" cause the subject to be treated as sui generis. The federal courts have a specifically prescribed and hence limited jurisdiction which occasions intricate problems as to the subject matter of their competence beyond the common problems of territoriality, service of process, in rem jurisdiction, and the like. Thus a federal court may also necessarily be concerned with whether an alleged cause of action arises out of the laws of the United States, whether there is the requisite diversity of citizenship, or whether the case is within the admiralty and maritime "federal jurisdiction." §§ 44–54.

12. *Erie* is within the ambit of the special problems of "federal jurisdiction." The obligation of federal courts in deciding civil actions is to follow the appropriate state law as the rule of

decision except where the Constitution, treaties or statutes of the United States otherwise require or provide. State law means judicial decisions as well as statutes. None of the attempts to work out a terminology for the Erie rubric, such as "substance" vs. "procedure" or "outcome determinative," have been completely satisfactory. Perhaps the most promising formula when federal "procedure" confronts state "substance" is that federal "courthouse" law governs the processes of the litigation but that state law governs "the primary decisions of human conduct."

13. The extraordinary relief available by the Great Writ of *habeas corpus* is subject to jurisdictional limitations based on territoriality. Other problems concerned with the operative scope of the writ are resolved in "jurisdictional" terms. § 55.

14. Jurisdictional concepts flourish in American *appellate* practice and procedure. The timely taking of the appeal is often "jurisdictional", in the sense that failure to act within the prescribed period of time precludes any consideration of the merits. This is rooted in the historic common law notion that appellate review is a proceeding separate and distinct from the trial court proceeding. This contrasts with the situation in modern England where appeals are by way of rehearing of trial court processes and hence analogous to equity review. § 56.

APPENDIX A

NEW YORK CIVIL PRACTICE LAW AND RULES (NY CPLR)

§ 301. Jurisdiction over persons, property or status

A court may exercise such jurisdiction over persons, property, or status as might have been exercised heretofore.

§ 302. Personal jurisdiction by acts of nondomiciliaries

(a) **Acts which are the basis of jurisdiction.** As to a cause of action arising from any of the acts enumerated in this section, a court may exercise personal jurisdiction over any nondomiciliary, or his executor or administrator, who in person or through an agent

1. transacts any business within the state; or

2. commits a tortious act within the state, except as to a cause of action for defamation of character arising from the act; or

3. commits a tortious act without the state causing injury to person or property within the state, except as to a cause of action for defamation of character arising from the act, if he

(i) regularly does or solicits business, or engages in any other persistent course of conduct, or derives substantial revenue from goods used or consumed or services rendered, in the state, or

(ii) expects or should reasonably expect the act to have consequences in the state and derives substantial revenue from interstate or international commerce; or

4. owns, uses or possesses any real property situated within the state.

(b) **Personal jurisdiction over non-resident defendant.** A court in any matrimonial action or family court proceeding involving a demand for support or alimony may exercise personal jurisdiction over the respondent or defendant notwithstanding the fact that he or she no longer is a resident or domiciliary of this state, or over his or her executor or administrator, if the party seeking support is a resident of or domiciled in this state at the time such demand is made, provided that this state was the matrimonial domicile of the parties before their separation, or the defendant abandoned the plaintiff in this state, or the obligation to pay support or alimony accrued under the laws of this state or under an agreement executed in this state.

(c) **Effect of appearance.** Where personal jurisdiction is based solely upon this section, an appearance does not confer such jurisdiction with respect to causes of action not arising from an act enumerated in this section.

§ 313. Service without the state giving personal jurisdiction

A person domiciled in the state or subject to the jurisdiction of the courts of the state under section 301 or 302, or his executor or administrator, may be served with the summons without the state, in the same manner as service is made within the state, by any person authorized to make service within the state who is a resident of the state or by any person authorized to make service by the laws of the state, territory, possession or country in which service is made or by any duly qualified attorney, solicitor, barrister, or equivalent in such jurisdiction.

§ 314. Service without the state not giving personal jurisdiction in certain actions

Service may be made without the state by any person authorized by section 313 in the same manner as service is made within the state:

1. in a matrimonial action; or

2. where a judgment is demanded that the person to be served be excluded from a vested or contingent interest in or lien upon specific real or personal property within the state; or that such an interest or lien in favor of either party be en-

forced, regulated, defined or limited; or otherwise affecting the title to such property, including an action of interpleader or defensive interpleader; or

3. where a levy upon property of the person to be served has been made within the state pursuant to an order of attachment or a chattel of such person has been seized in an action to recover a chattel.

§ 315. **Service by publication authorized**

The court, upon motion without notice, shall order service of a summons by publication in an action described in section 314 if service cannot be made by another prescribed method with due diligence.

APPENDIX B

FEDERAL RULES OF CIVIL PROCEDURE

Rule 4.

PROCESS

(a) Summons: Issuance. Upon the filing of the complaint the clerk shall forthwith issue a summons and deliver it for service to the marshal or to a person specially appointed to serve it. Upon request of the plaintiff separate or additional summons shall issue against any defendants.

(b) Same: Form. The summons shall be signed by the clerk, be under the seal of the court, contain the name of the court and the names of the parties, be directed to the defendant, state the name and address of the plaintiff's attorney, if any, otherwise the plaintiff's address, and the time within which these rules require the defendant to appear and defend, and shall notify him that in case of his failure to do so judgment by default will be rendered against him for the relief demanded in the complaint. When, under Rule 4(e), service is made pursuant to a statute or rule of court of a state, the summons, or notice, or order in lieu of summons shall correspond as nearly as may be to that required by the statute or rule.

(c) By Whom Served. Service of all process shall be made by a United States marshal, by his deputy, or by some person specially appointed by the court for that purpose, except that a subpoena may be served as provided in Rule 45. Special appointments to serve process shall be made freely when substantial savings in travel fees will result.

(d) Summons: Personal Service. The summons and complaint shall be served together. The plaintiff shall furnish the person making service with such copies as are necessary. Service shall be made as follows:

(1) Upon an individual other than an infant or an incompetent person, by delivering a copy of the summons and of the complaint to him personally or by leaving copies thereof at his dwelling house or usual place of abode with some person of suitable age and discretion then residing therein or by delivering a copy of the summons and of the complaint to an agent authorized by appointment or by law to receive service of process.

(2) Upon an infant or an incompetent person, by serving the summons and complaint in the manner prescribed by the law of the state in which the service is made for the service of summons or other like process upon any such defend-

ant in an action brought in the courts of general jurisdiction of that state.

(3) Upon a domestic or foreign corporation or upon a partnership or other unincorporated association which is subject to suit under a common name, by delivering a copy of the summons and of the complaint to an officer, a managing or general agent, or to any other agent authorized by appointment or by law to receive service of process and, if the agent is one authorized by statute to receive service and the statute so requires, by also mailing a copy to the defendant.

(4) Upon the United States, by delivering a copy of the summons and of the complaint to the United States attorney for the district in which the action is brought or to an assistant United States attorney or clerical employee designated by the United States attorney in a writing filed with the clerk of the court and by sending a copy of the summons and of the complaint by registered or certified mail to the Attorney General of the United States at Washington, District of Columbia, and in any action attacking the validity of an order of an officer or agency of the United States not made a party, by also sending a copy of the summons and of the complaint by registered or certified mail to such officer or agency.

(5) Upon an officer or agency of the United States, by serving the United States and by de-

livering a copy of the summons and of the complaint to such officer or agency. If the agency is a corporation the copy shall be delivered as provided in paragraph (3) of this subdivision of this rule.

(6) Upon a state or municipal corporation or other governmental organization thereof subject to suit, by delivering a copy of the summons and of the complaint to the chief executive officer thereof or by serving the summons and complaint in the manner prescribed by the law of that state for the service of summons or other like process upon any such defendant.

(7) Upon a defendant of any class referred to in paragraph (1) or (3) of this subdivision of this rule, it is also sufficient if the summons and complaint are served in the manner prescribed by any statute of the United States or in the manner prescribed by the law of the state in which the district court is held for the service of summons or other like process upon any such defendant in an action brought in the courts of general jurisdiction of that state.

(e) Same: Service Upon Party Not Inhabitant of or Found Within State. Whenever a statute of the United States or an order of court thereunder provides for service of a summons, or of a notice, or of an order in lieu of summons upon a party not an inhabitant of or found within the state in which the district court is held, service may be made under the circumstances and in the manner prescribed by the statute or order, or, if there is no provision therein prescribing the manner of service, in a manner stated in this rule. Whenever a statute or rule of court of the state in which the district court is held provides (1) for service of a summons, or a notice, or of an order in lieu of summons upon a party not an inhabitant of or found within the state, or (2) for service upon or notice to him to appear and respond or defend in an action by reason of the attachment or garnishment or similar seizure of his property located within the state, service may in either case be made under the circumstances and in the manner prescribed in the statute or rule.

(f) Territorial Limits of Effective Service. All process other than a subpoena may be served anywhere within the territorial limits of the state in which the district court is held, and, when authorized by a statute of the United States or by these rules, beyond the territorial limits of that state. In addition, persons who are brought in as parties pursuant to Rule 14, or as additional parties to a pending action or a counterclaim or cross-claim therein pursuant to Rule 19, may be served in the manner stated in paragraphs (1)–(6) of subdivision (d) of this rule at all places outside the state but within the United States that are not more than 100 miles from the place in which the action is commenced, or to which it is assigned or transferred for trial; and persons required to respond to an order of commitment for civil contempt may be served at the same places. A subpoena may be served within the territorial limits provided in Rule 45.

(g) Return. The person serving the process shall make proof of service thereof to the court promptly and in any event within the time during which the person served must respond to the process. If service is made by a person other than a United States marshal or his deputy, he shall make affidavit thereof. Failure to make proof of service does not affect the validity of the service.

(h) Amendment. At any time in it discretion and upon such terms as it deems just, the court may allow any process or proof of service thereof to be amended, unless it clearly appears that material prejudice would result to the substantial rights of the party against whom the process issued.

(i) Alternative Provisions for Service in a Foreign Country.

(1) Manner. When the federal or state law referred to in subdivision (e) of this rule authorizes service upon a party not an inhabitant of or found within the state in which the district court is held, and service is to be effected upon the par-

ty in a foreign country, it is also sufficient if service of the summons and complaint is made: (A) in the manner prescribed by the law of the foreign country for service in that country in an action in any of its courts of general jurisdiction; or (B) as directed by the foreign authority in response to a letter rogatory, when service in either case is reasonably calculated to give actual notice; or (C) upon an individual, by delivery to him personally, and upon a corporation or partnership or association, by delivery to an officer, a managing or general agent; or (D) by any form of mail, requiring a signed receipt, to be addressed and dispatched by the clerk of the court to the party to be served; or (E) as directed by order of the court. Service under (C) or (E) above may be made by any person who is not a party and is not less than 18 years of age or who is designated by order of the district court or by the foreign court. On request, the clerk shall deliver the summons to the plaintiff for transmission to the person or the foreign court or officer who will make the service.

(2) Return. Proof of service may be made as prescribed by subdivision (g) of this rule, or by the law of the foreign country, or by order of the court. When service is made pursuant to subparagraph (1) (D) of this subdivision, proof of service shall include a receipt signed by the addressee

or other evidence of delivery to the addressee satisfactory to the court.

(As amended Jan. 21, 1963, eff. July 1, 1963; Feb. 28, 1966, eff. July 1, 1966.)

Rule 12.

DEFENSES AND OBJECTIONS—WHEN AND HOW PRESENTED—BY PLEADING OR MOTION—MOTION FOR JUDGMENT ON PLEADINGS

(a) When Presented. A defendant shall serve his answer within 20 days after the service of the summons and complaint upon him, except when service is made under Rule 4(e) and a different time is prescribed in the order of court under the statute of the United States or in the statute or rule of court of the state. A party served with a pleading stating a cross-claim against him shall serve an answer thereto within 20 days after the service upon him. The plaintiff shall serve his reply to a counterclaim in the answer within 20 days after service of the answer or, if a reply is ordered by the court, within 20 days after service of the order, unless the order otherwise directs. The United States or an officer or agency thereof shall serve an answer to the complaint or to a cross-claim, or a reply to a counterclaim, within 60 days after the service upon the United States attorney of the pleading in which the claim is asserted. The service of a motion permitted under this rule alters these periods to time as follows, unless a different time is fixed by order of the court: (1) if the court denies the motion or postpones its disposition until the trial on the merits, the responsive pleading shall be served within 10 days after notice of the court's action; (2) if the court grants a motion for a more definite statement the responsive pleading shall be served within 10 days after the service of the more definite statement.

(b) **How Presented.** Every defense, in law or fact, to a claim for relief in any pleading, whether a claim, counterclaim, cross-claim, or third-party claim, shall be asserted in the responsive pleading thereto if one is required, except that the following defenses may at the option of the pleader be made by motion: (1) lack of jurisdiction over the subject matter, (2) lack of jurisdiction over the person, (3) improper venue, (4) insufficiency of process, (5) insufficiency of service of process, (6) failure to state a claim upon which relief can be granted, (7) failure to join a party under Rule 19. A motion making any of these defenses shall be made before pleading if a further pleading is permitted. No defense or objection is waived by being joined with one or more other defenses or objections in a responsive pleading or motion. If a pleading sets forth a claim for relief to which the adverse party is not required to serve a responsive pleading, he may assert at the trial any defense in law or fact to that claim for relief. If, on a motion asserting the defense numbered (6) to dismiss for failure of the pleading to state a claim upon which relief can be granted, matters outside the pleading are presented to and not excluded by the court, the motion shall be treated as one for summary judgment and disposed of as provided in Rule 56, and all parties shall be given reasonable opportunity to present all material made pertinent to such a motion by Rule 56.

(c) Motion for Judgment on the Pleadings. After the pleadings are closed but within such time as not to delay the trial, any party may move for judgment on the pleadings. If, on a motion for judgment on the pleadings, matters outside the pleadings are presented to and not excluded by the court, the motion shall be treated as one for summary judgment and disposed of as provided in Rule 56, and all parties shall be given reasonable opportunity to present all material made pertinent to such a motion by Rule 56.

(d) Preliminary Hearings. The defenses specifically enumerated (1)–(7) in subdivision (b) of this rule, whether made in a pleading or by motion, and the motion for judgment mentioned in subdivision (c) of this rule shall be heard and determined before trial on application of any party, unless the court orders that the hearing and determination thereof be deferred until the trial.

(e) Motion for More Definite Statement. If a pleading to which a responsive pleading is permitted is so vague or ambiguous that a party cannot reasonably be required to frame a responsible pleading, he may move for a more definite statement before interposing his responsible pleadings. The motion shall point out the defects complained of and the details desired. If the motion is granted and the order of the court is not obeyed within 10 days after notice of the order or within such other time as the court may fix, the court may strike the pleading to which the motion was directed or make such order as it deems just.

(f) Motion To Strike. Upon motion made by a party before responding to a pleading or, if no responsive pleading is permitted by these rules, upon motion made by a party within 20 days after the service of the pleading upon him or upon the court's own initiative at any time, the court may order stricken from any pleading any insufficient defense or any redundant, immaterial, impertinent, or scandalous matter.

(g) Consolidation of Defenses in Motion. A party who makes a motion under this rule may join with it any other motions herein provided for and then available to him. If a party makes a motion under this rule but omits therefrom any defense or objection then available to him which this rule permits to be raised by motion, he shall not thereafter make a motion based on the defense or objection so omitted, except a motion as provided in subdivision (h)(2) hereof on any of the grounds there stated.

(h) Waiver of Preservation of Certain Defenses.

(1) A defense of lack of jurisdiction over the person, improper venue, insufficiency of process, or insufficiency of service of process is waived (A) if omitted from a motion in the circumstances described in subdivision (g), or (B) if it is neither made by motion under this rule nor included in a responsive pleading or an amendment thereof permitted by Rule 15(a) to be made as a matter of course.

(2) A defense of failure to state a claim upon which relief can be granted, a defense of failure to join a party indispensable under Rule 19, and an objection of failure to state a legal defense to a claim may be made in any pleading permitted or ordered under Rule 7(a), or by motion for judgment on the pleadings, or at the trial on the merits.

(3) Whenever it appears by suggestion of the parties or otherwise that the court lacks jurisdic-

tion of the subject matter, the court shall dismiss the action.

(As amended Dec. 27, 1946, eff. Mar. 19, 1948; Jan. 21, 1963, eff. July 1, 1963; Feb. 28, 1966, eff. July 1, 1966.)

Rule 19.

JOINDER OF PERSONS NEEDED FOR JUST ADJUDICATION

(a) Persons To Be Joined if Feasible. A person who is subject to service of process and whose joinder will not deprive the court of jurisdiction over the subject matter of the action shall be joined as party in the action if (1) in his absence complete relief cannot be accorded among those already parties, or (2) he claims an interest relating to the subject of the action and is so situated that the disposition of the action in his absence may (i) as a practical matter impair or impede his ability to protect that interest or (ii) leave any of the persons already parties subject to a substantial risk of incurring double, multiple, or otherwise inconsistent obligations by reason of his claimed interest. If he has not been so joined, the court shall order that he be made a party. If he should join as a plaintiff but refuses to do so, he may be made a defendant, or, in a proper case, an involuntary plaintiff. If the joined party objects to venue and his joinder would render the venue of the action improper, he shall be dismissed from the action.

(b) Determination by Court Whenever Joinder Not Feasible. If a person as described in subdivision (a)(1)–(2) hereof cannot be made a party, the court shall determine whether in equity and good conscience the action should proceed among the parties before it, or should be dismissed, the absent person being thus regarded as indispensable. The factors to be considered by the court include: first, to what extent a judgment rendered in the person's absence might be prejudicial to him or those already parties; second, the extent to which, by protective provisions in the judgment, by the shaping of relief, or other measures, the prejudice can be lessened or avoided; third, whether a judgment rendered in the person's absence will be adequate; fourth, whether the plaintiff will have an adequate remedy if the action is dismissed for nonjoinder.

(c) Pleading Reasons for Nonjoinder. A pleading asserting a claim for relief shall state the names, if known to the pleader, of any persons as described in subdivision (a)(1)–(2) hereof who are not joined, and the reasons why they are not joined.

(d) Exception of Class Actions. This rule is subject to the provisions of Rule 23.

(As amended Feb. 28, 1966, eff. July 1, 1966.)

INDEX

References are to Pages

A

INDEX

References are to Pages

INDEX

References are to Pages

INDEX

References are to Pages

INDEX

References are to Pages

B

C

INDEX

References are to Pages

INDEX

References are to Pages

INDEX

References are to Pages

INDEX

References are to Pages

INDEX

References are to Pages

G

H

J

L

INDEX

References are to Pages

M

N

V

W

‡